Our Dance Through Life

Volume 2

GURMEET K DHANJAL
NUSOUND RADIO LISTENERS
ARIA DHANJAL

Our Dance Through Life (Vol 2)

Copyright © 2021: Gurmeet Dhanjal

All rights reserved. No part of this publication may be produced, distributed, or transmitted in any form or by any means, including photocopying, recording, or other electronic or mechanical methods, without the prior written permission of the publisher, except in the case of brief quotations embodied in critical reviews and certain other non-commercial uses permitted by copyright law.

First Printed in United Kingdom 2021

Published by Conscious Dreams Publishing
www.consciousdreamspublishing.com

Edited by Elise Abram
Typeset by Amit Dey

ISBN: 978-1-913674-76-2 (Paperback)

Dedication

I dedicate this book to all who are no longer with us,
to those who are in recovery, to those that are living
a life of service, to those that are just surviving,
to those who are thriving, and to everybody
in between.

When everything else is taken from us, and we have nothing left, we still have our imaginations to take us places, revisit experiences, plan better futures, and sow new seeds in our minds for a brighter tomorrow. By the grace of God, all will be just as it is meant to be.

Sikh Mool Mantra
ਮੂਲ ਮੰਤਰ
मूल मंतर

੧ੳ	Ek Omkaar
ਸਤਿ ਨਾਮੁ	Sat Naam
ਕਰਤਾ ਪੁਰਖੁ	Karta Purakh
ਨਿਰਭਉ ਨਿਰਵੈਰੁ	Nirbhau Nirvair
ਅਕਾਲ ਮੂਰਤਿ	Akaal Muurat
ਅਜੂਨੀ ਸੈਭੰ	Ajooni Saibhang
ਗੁਰ ਪ੍ਰਸਾਦਿ ॥	Guru Prasaad

The One Reality and Source of everything,
The True Name,
The Supreme Person Who is the Creator and Doer of everything,
Devoid of fear and devoid of enmity,
The Timeless Form of the Supreme,
The Self-Existent One beyond birth,
by the Grace of Guru.

Jayamithram Sarvada

This is the Sikh Mool Mantar, taken from the Sikh Holy Scripture called 'Sri Guru Granth Sahib', which is the longest poetry book ever written. Each verse can be recited and sung to different ragas (Indian musical notes). The Mool Mantar is a reminder of the ever-present Universe, who is ultimately in control of everything that happens on this earth and beyond. My inspiration for poetry is derived from these verses.

Contents

Preface xiii

Chapter 1: Gurmeet Kaur Dhanjal 1
1 Ek-Onkar. 5
2 I Die Each Day. 6
3 Dahlia. 8
4 Husband 10
5 My Wife 12
6 A Good Wife 14
7 Survival. 17
8 Traditions. 18
9 Autumn. 21
10 Windy Days 22
11 Early Morning Walk 24
12 Feeling the Loss. 27
13 How to Keep your Husband/Wife. 30
14 Lockdown, Lockdown 34

15 School Days 37
16 To My Papa 39
17 Reaching for the Stars 41
18 My Perfect Valentine 43
19 Sir Tom 44
20 Evils of this World 46
21 A Modern Family 48
22 Exceptional Parenting 51
23 Going our Separate Ways 53
24 Happiness is Being Served 55
25 Bud 57
26 Night Sky 59
27 Friends 60
28 Trolling 62
29 Snow 64
30 WhatsApp 66
31 Old is Gold 69
32 Life Interrupted 71
33 Washing Up 73
34 The Golden Years 75
35 My Knitting Needles 78
36 Paronthas 80
37 Valentine's Day 82

38 Oh Christmas Tree 84
39 The Waiting Game 86
40 NuSound Radio. 88
41 Enough 90
42 Farmers 92
43 Puddles 95
44 Mother Earth 97
45 Hands 100
46 Water 102
47 Rules. 104
48 Found 106
49 The Crow 107
50 Pride. 109
51 Forgiveness 110
52 The Sun 111
53 Diet 112
54 Pushing Boundaries. 114
55 Reading Club 116
56 Gardening. 118
57 Goodbye, *AuRevoir*, Sat Sri Akal 120
58 Cleaning. 121
59 Loneliness. 123
60 Homelessness 125

61 The Royal Family 127

62 Now that you are Gone. 129

63 Now that you are Back 130

64 The Weather Man. 131

65 To Feel Alive 132

66 When Two Hearts Meet 134

67 You are not Alone 136

68 Ghosts of the Past 137

69 Ardaas. 139

70 What Mama Never Told Me 140

71 I am a Bottle 142

72 Ageing. 143

73 5 K's of Sikhism. 145

74 I am a Tree 149

75 Silence. 151

76 My Silence. 153

Chapter 2: NuSound Radio Listeners. 155

77 Traveller By Night 159

78 Balance 160

79 COVID-19 161

80 Leading Up to Mother's Day 164

81 Fragrance of Spring. 166

82 LOOK 168
83 Note to My Younger Self. 169
84 The Queue 170
85 I am a Woman 172
86 Somewhere 173
87 Happy International Women's Day. 174
88 Love not Hate. 175
89 Fighting the Coronavirus 176
90 Happy Days will Bloom and Blossom 178
91 Courage 180
92 Mum's Cooking 181
93 Just Food 182
94 The Beauty of Snow 183
95 Dear COVID 184
96 The Necklace 185
97 Souvenir. 186
98 Holi 188
99 Gauri 190
100 Battle of the Spices 192

Chapter 3: Aria K Dhanjal **193**
101 Spring 195
102 Snow 196

103 Presents 197
104 Christmas Tree. 198
105 Lockdown 199
106 Walk Through the Forest 200
107 Friendship 201
108 Homeschooling 202
109 Winter 203
110 At Grandmother's House 204
111 The Coming of the Iron Man 206
112 People Need People 208

Acknowledgements 210
About the Author 212
Aria Dhanjal 213
Other Books by Gurmeet Dhanjal 214
Book Reviews 215

Preface

2020, was a poignant year for many different reasons, personally, as my husband and I began to enjoy our retired life to the worldwide politics. The UK left the EU, Harry and Meghan made their departure from the royal family, President Trump was voted out, and India became a battleground for farmers and its government.

Most importantly, 2020 would be remembered for COVID-19 and the devastation it left. Many businesses went bankrupt, and life as we knew it was put on hold. Holiday restrictions meant people were unable to travel abroad, and nationwide lockdowns left many stranded in their homes to fend for themselves.

In one way or another, COVID-19 affected the lives of all worldwide, from contracting the virus to losing loved ones. Different sources reported that there were more deaths recorded from COVID-19 than people killed in WW2 or WW1. To add to the stress of loss, people were not permitted to say goodbye to their loved ones or be at their bedsides as they recovered from the virus. As a result, many were left emotionally and mentally exhausted, and there was increased anxiety based on the uncertainty of jobs, schooling, and performing normal recreational activities.

Everybody played their parts in seeing us through this extraordinary year, from handing out food parcels to getting people exercising and finding some comfort in singing.

I wanted to play my part in helping. The success and sense of achievement of my first book spurred me to write a sequel to capture the feelings and experiences of people through poetry, but how I would do this was still a question in my mind.

As we continue with our journeys on this earth, we discover new things, new experiences, and feelings we haven't felt before. We discover that things are forever changing around us over which we have no control, but we have the resilience to get through them together, bonded by the commonalities of love and compassion.

On a personal level, I felt if I could get people inspired to write, it would be an opportunity for me to help them deal with their feelings of life during lockdown.

The Universe was listening and acquainted me with a wonderful person named Mohni, who happened to be a radio presenter at NuSound Radio.

My journey to radio:

My journey to NuSound radio started by chance on Women's International Day when a celebration was organised by the

Labour Party. I happened to be invited. On the invitation, there was a call for people to share and celebrate their achievements. Having just published my book called 'Our Dance Through Life' during autumn of 2019, I thought I would take a few copies to hand out to whoever wanted one. There were many important people in attendance, like Councillor Jaz Atwal, other poets, singers, dancers, and radio presenters. It so happened that I ended up standing next to one of the NuSound Radio's presenters, munching away on our sandwiches. I introduced myself, handing her a copy of my book and offering to appear on her show if she wanted me to talk about it. Yes, you guessed it right: her name was Mohni. Later that evening, we were both going to another event, so I offered to give her a lift. Our friendship had started, and I looked eagerly forward to how it would unfold.

Then, one day, I got a message from Mohni to say she was so impressed with my book that she wanted to get me on her show. Soon after, we had a lockdown because of COVID-19, so I was invited to call in as a listener to share my poems. Each week, I shared a poem from my book and talked about the inspiration behind it. The response from the public was overwhelming. Many listeners were moved by the experiences of life on which I touched, and the feedback was always positive. I found this very reassuring and became comfortable listening to myself on the radio.

The situation with COVID-19 was getting dire, and people were looking for some form of escape, so I decided to sponsor an hour-long breakfast primetime show every Tuesday from nine to ten, sharing, discussing, and encouraging people to get writing. The radio show reached listeners as far as India, Australia, and America, who were inspired to start writing their own stories in the form of poems. These are now included in this book. Many more have started on their journeys, but they are not yet confident to share them.

This book is very much a reflection of what was going through people's minds and hearts in 2020. It's a symbol of survival, companionship, support, laughter, and love that saw us through a tough year in history. Teamwork and the recognition of each other's efforts inspired and motivated us and kept our spirits lifted through the grey skies of winter and sunnier days of summer.

Finally, writing this book has been like painting a picture on a blank canvas—we started with nothing and yet, managed to create a beautiful piece of art through everybody's poetry of personal journeys to be enjoyed by all.

The proceeds from the sale of this book will go towards 'Khalsa Aid', a charity close to my heart for a lot of different reasons, set up by Ravi Singh, CEO, who has been nominated for this year's Nobel Peace Prize for his efforts in helping people all over the world with his team of volunteers. They have managed to help and support people in the remotest parts of the world under extreme conditions, often at the risk of losing their own lives to fulfil the basic needs of others, such as food, clothes, and medicine, without which people would die.

The positive side of COVID

There have been many positives during the last year, as well. For instance, if COVID hadn't happened, this book would not have been published. I would not have been a part of the awesome radio community. We wouldn't have known about the talent of so many different writers showcased in this book. COVID, in my eyes, also broke down the barriers of culture and religious differences, as everybody became immersed in helping each other.

Personally, I have become more relaxed being in my own body, and I tend to pace myself by doing new projects. I have become better at articulating my feelings verbally without fear. I now choose to focus only on the positive traits of people and not dwell on their weaknesses. Nobody is perfect, and we all make mistakes. I have learnt to let go of a lot of things that no longer seem important in the context of the year we had. I am making it my mission to live a life of forgiveness and gratitude as we are the lucky ones who have survived. Lastly, I have learnt to live in the moment rather than worrying about the past or the future and enjoy each day as it comes.

'Amar Writers' Award'

As I continued to write, it was hard for me to know how to get my work published, as no one in my family had ever been down this route. It was something that others did, and we dared to imagine ourselves as writers, but where there is a will, there's a way. Through a friend who had just published her book, I discovered that I, too, could get my poems published. These poems were

20 years' worth of work. and I did not want to lose what I had written. I wanted to set an example for my children that anything is possible if you really want it.

One day, as I did with all of my poems, I forwarded one of them to a friend. She read the poem and simply said, 'Gurmeet, why don't you get them published?' to which I replied, 'Give me the name of your publisher,' which she did. It still took another year for me to pluck up the courage and find a way to forward the poems to the brilliant Conscious Dreams Publishing, its CEO, Danni Blechner, and her team, who read the poems and said, 'We love your poems and will publish them.'

This was so exciting for my family and me. My children helped me decide how I should lay the book out, and it was their idea for me to include photos of my life to reflect the people mentioned in my poems. Wow! I was the first published author in my family, and it felt great.

I then had a reflective moment when I realised that all of my achievements would not have been possible if it weren't for the sacrifices made by my parents, giving up their opportunities to provide for us. My father was illiterate and would sign his name with the first and last letter of his name. He had to ask friends and relatives to read any correspondence he received from his family in India. I felt that these amazing people should be honoured and not forgotten, so when I got my book published, I felt there must be so many people like me who have the talent but lacked self-belief and the knowledge about how to share their work with the world. To that end, I decided to set up the

Amar Writers' Award to honour my father and mother who gave their nine children the grounding to be who we are today. I imagined going into secondary schools to set up a competition for children to enter, from which I would choose the best story and get it published, but lockdown changed all that, so I took another route, which was to go on the radio and inspire people to write. I did not go in with the intention of getting a book out of the experience, but the Universe had other plans. The response was 'Phenomenal'— the word used by the CEO of the radio station. I couldn't think of worthier recipients to earn my first award than the listeners and the presenters.

It is with the utmost privilege that I give my first award to NuSound Radio and its listeners for helping me write this book. Upon the release of this book, the award will be handed over to them ceremonially.

Each year, I will seek out writers to publish their very first books while keeping the legacy of my father going.

I survived yesterday, I am dealing with today, I will face tomorrow and whatever comes my way with love, courage and compassion, but live my life in service to others is what gives it real meaning and satisfaction.

CHAPTER 1

Gurmeet Kaur Dhanjal

In this chapter, I explore the ever-changing nature of relationships in the present climate, how each relationship has a ripple effect on all the people concerned in a household, and how we fight through the changes by trying to make sense of what's happened and why, as well as the feelings that arise because of the decisions people make due to their personal circumstances.

More and more, relationships end in separation or divorce nowadays. No culture or religious group is immune to the changing shift in relationships. Generally, people are less tolerant and more focused on their own life's journeys. As a result of this, the effects felt by some people are irreversible, often ending in mental breakdown and depression, and in some cases, suicide, when there isn't the family support to see them through the changes.

Relationships, per my understanding, are habits you develop between different people. These become a way of carrying the relationship forward. The habits you develop may be those that bring out the best or the worst in people. Once you are in this pattern, you become emotionally attached through the feelings it evokes in you. While some habits can be detrimental to your spiritual, professional, and personal development, other relationships can be sources of inspiration and encouragement, helping you to progress and succeed in all areas of your life. The latter can be classed as a good working relationship.

When you become aware of detrimental relationships, there are two choices you have: physical detachment that leads to living independent lives from each other by moving out of the home you share; or mentally detaching yourself from the person and beginning to make small changes in already established habits to let the other person know you are not happy with things, and changes have to take place in order for the relationship to survive. If both people are in it for the long haul, they will respect, listen, and make the changes. If two people are not willing to listen to each other and they are too embedded in their ways to want to change, then that relationship will not survive.

Often, it is the insecurities of people and the fear that they may lose their identities that lead to them digging in their heels.

Our identities are what we give ourselves. Our identities change as we grow through the different roles we play at work and with our friends and the new relationships we develop, but our souls are always the same. The world is our stage. We are mere actors playing different roles on this vast stage called life. Sometimes we get stuck in a role and begin to think that this is who we are but no; We are all spiritual beings in physical form on our soul journeys, playing different roles. Like the actors on a stage, we have to make exits from some roles in order to make space for new ones to develop, but it is difficult to sever relationships completely as you may need them in your life at another day and time, especially if there are children involved.

In my experience, human relationships are the same, but people's reactions to them have changed as the roles of men and women have evolved. In the past, women and men had clear-cut roles to play in a family, with the men being the main breadwinners and the women the housekeepers who were responsible for the upbringing of children. Today, in some cases, the roles have reversed, and there is more freedom to live independently and move from relationship to relationship until the perfect partner comes on the scene.

In the first chapter, my poems reflect my relationships with my husband and the people around me. Some people have exited my life because of the pain, hurt, and control they brought into my life, which was suffocating and hindered my growth, while new people have entered into my life to enrich it with love and encouragement to help me find my true purpose.

One thing that has never changed in my life is the constant belief that everything is happening for my higher good and the faith that it is all working out just as it was meant to be. Through daily meditation, I find solutions to all my problems. I now know that every problem has a solution; you just have to dig deep to find it, and in time, things will eventually fall into place despite everything.

The latter part of the chapter reflects my inner peace and some understanding of the powers at work in our lives. The more time I spend with nature, the closer I feel to my grave. This is our reality. One day we all have to exit from this earth, so I have chosen to live my life free of fear, welcome the challenges that give me purpose, and strive to move forward each day. With this understanding, I am now driven by what really matters to me, and I tackle it with gusto and give it the pure energy it deserves without any fear of loss or failure. It is what it is. I now live my life in gratitude for all that was, all that is, and all that will be in the future. I have no expectations and receive what comes to me happily, whatever it may be. I have learnt to forgive my past, and I am in awe of the future that is being carved for me. I wake up in gratitude and go to bed in gratitude.

In between, there are, of course, poems reflecting the mood of 2020, the lockdown, and COVID with which we had to contend, and the heroic acts of kindness displayed by ordinary people while across the world, people had to deal with challenges of different kinds, which also caught my eye.

1
Ek-Onkar

The Eternal light
Consciousness
Self-Existence
Eternal Truth
Ever-Present
All-Knowing
Nameless
Universal
Protector
Supreme
Formless
Timeless
Fearless
Forgiver
Creator
Loving
Mother
Father
Divine
GOD

By Gurmeet Dhanjal

2
I Die Each Day

I die each day
Then I find a reason to stay
Since being born one sunny day
When I was little
I got told I was no good
I tried anyway and got through school
I got told I couldn't
I went to college and became a teacher
I got told don't dream
I found myself a husband
I got told I was weak
I gave myself a family of three children
I got told life was full of misery
I created life full of things that made me happy
I got told I was fat and ugly
I fed myself good food wore beautiful clothes
I looked in the face of adversity
And turned things around
Then one dark gloomy day
My thoughts turned on me
The thoughts of ending my life
Became tempting

I felt like I was sinking in quicksand
But my inner-strength took over
I began to put the negative thoughts away
My time was not yet up
I had everything to live for
I still had a lot to achieve
People to inspire
I prayed to GOD that he would let me know
when my time was up
I would drift away
Without a fight
In my sleep I will go one day
But for now, I am here to stay

By Gurmeet Dhanjal

3
Dahlia

Dahlia, the queen of the garden
You come in all different
Colours, shapes, and sizes
Red with white tips
Burgundy all round and perfect
With purple, tiny, close-knit petals
You are the surprise my eyes yearn to see
With perfect yellow like the sun
Each morning I kneel before you
And give you a kiss
For in you I see the beauty
Of a lover I want to cherish
From tiny little tubers
You did grow
Into a majestic plant
That towers above the rest
Still standing tall
Having stood the test
Of drought, extreme heat
Still, your beauty can never be beat
My dahlia queen of the flowers

By Gurmeet Dhanjal

Poems 4 and 5 were prompted by the voice of the wife inside of me who has carried out her duties in silence as required in an extended family without ever asking for anything in return, trying to maintain a happy family, putting on many faces but never the one that shows her true feelings.

In poem 4, she is questioning her husband, who shares her bed and sees her every day, but he never bothers to ask what she desires, if she is happy, or to celebrate her achievements, simply show any kind of recognition of her presence in his life, or help deal with challenging situations when they arrive.

In poem 5, she has answered her own questions based on her perception of the person he is and his limiting but simple way of life that stops him from digging deep into his or anybody else's feelings, supporting her in his own way by silently being there through thick and thin. She appreciates that she is responsible for her own happiness while he seeks his own in the best way he knows how.

4
Husband

My husband of yesterday
You are still the same
Handsome man I married, today!
Then why is it
That I don't feel the same way?
Is it because we have
Both travelled our
Separate ways too far
The understanding
We had of each other
Is no longer there
I try so hard to come close
Only to feel repelled
You never ask why
Turn the other way and say goodbye
Do you not see
That things are not the same
Or do you choose
To ignore and carry on?
Afraid of the answers
You may hear
One day you will

That day is near
I want a husband
Who has an ear for me
Or the yesteryears
Would have had no meaning at all
We have so much to share
While sitting in our rocking chairs
My heart yearns to feel
Loved again and travel down memory lane
Where we shared a hug and a kiss
Looked into each other's eyes with desire
Big things like a car
And holidays matter no more
It's the touch and a smile
That is worth so much more
My husband of yesterday
Do you remember at all
Or is it my fantasy
That we shared a life together
And there is nothing
To it at all?

By Gurmeet Dhanjal

5
My Wife

My dearest wife of yesteryears
I hear your cries and feel your pain
Standing right here beside you
Watching you endure
Pains of motherhood you chose
It wasn't easy but there was nothing I could do
For the journey was yours to travel
Love I tried to show
You found hard to receive
So I gave you space instead
Until you were ready for me again
Time and time you pushed me away
But my love for you kept me right here beside you
A brave face I did show
In your silence you know
Trying to understand
The person stood in front of me
Whom I didn't know
My wife of yesteryears
Was gentle, strong, and determined
Now I see someone
Who has weathered the storms

But still looks beautiful
Wearing the wrinkles of life
With pride and joy
My wife of today
I love you more then
I did yesterday
I am here always beside you still
Your husband of yesterday!

By Gurmeet Dhanjal

6
A Good Wife

'You are a good wife,' he said
While giving her a hug
As she organises the family's events
Washes dishes, and keeps the house clean,
Cooks fresh food for family and friends
Puts on a big smile while looking her best

'You are a good wife,' he said
You gave me a family
Two boys and a girl
Now I have parents' evenings to attend
Special assemblies to watch
Entertain kids on special birthdays

'You are a good wife,' he said
I can hold my head up high in society
Boast of the big house I have
The posh car I drive
The degrees my kids have achieved
Now weddings to organise

'You are a good wife,' he said

'I am a good wife,' I said
Where were you
When I was crying during the night
Full of insecurities?
Where were you
When the kids needed discipline
And I on my knees
With despair?
Where were you
When I felt broke?

'Yes, I am a good wife,' I said
Are you even aware of the person I am
Of my dreams and desires
Things I want to achieve?
I came to this earth
With a soul purpose
I need time now to fulfil that for sure
For I have no desire to
Visit this earth again!

'Yes, I am a good wife,' I said
Let me be free of bondage
Of relations and my duties
Let me be free to express myself
In ways I never knew I could
Let me be free to fly

To soar the limitless skies above
Let me be me!
'Yes, I have been a good wife,' I said
But now I am free

By Gurmeet Dhanjal

7
Survival

Survival is the name of the game
The name of the game is life
With the very first breath you take
The battle to survive begins
You are dealt the cards
The scene is set
Choose your moves carefully
Read your opponent's mind
Then make your move
With a bit of luck
And shrewdness
You have the advantage
No time to be complacent
Or soak in the glory
Start thinking about your next move
Don't look left or right
Keep your sight set on the prize
If you make a mistake
Don't wallow in your sorrows
Get up and start again
Survival is the name of the game
The name of the game is Life!

By Gurmeet Dhanjal

8
Traditions

Traditions are the stepping-stones of life
Laid down one day a long time ago
By the forefathers and the friends
Time to do things together
Laugh, joke, and play
As a way of forgetting
The toll and sweat
Gone into earning daily bread
Roof over their heads
Clothes to cover
The naked bodies

Traditions are the stepping-stones of life
To give thanks
For the gift of a family
Children and friends
Who come into our lives
For support on days
Of happiness, sadness and grieving too
To share the laughter
Of weddings, birthdays

And graduations of few
That lead to jobs new

Traditions are the stepping-stones of life
To remember the sacrifice
Made by the brave crew
A legacy of bravery
Shown in best possible way
Their stories we do remember
With a tear in our eyes
Who were these people
Who sacrificed their lives for free
Angels from above
Sent down for me?

Traditions are the stepping-stones of life
Days to look forward to
Special clothes to wear
Makeup and hair
Invitations to write
Food to plan
Ingredients to buy
With the money put aside
For a purpose
To spread joy and happiness
With people I call mine

Traditions are the stepping-stones of life
Without them what would you do?
Sit alone with nothing to do
Watch TV and bore your mind too
Nothing to look forward to
No joy to spread
No laughter to share
You sit alone reminiscing
Of the traditions of the past
That brought you
Close to people
That no longer exist
With them died the traditions and all!

By Gurmeet Dhanjal

9
Autumn

Autumn, season of colour
Full of festival lights
Diwali, Hanukkah, and Bonfire nights
Time for celebrations, eating, laughing, and fighting.

Leaves falling
Squirrels scurrying
Collecting acorns
Happily burying

Rainy days
Umbrellas out
Of all colours, shapes, sizes on display
Children kicking and splashing puddles in a big way

Autumn leaves, orange, red, brown, and yellow
Feeding the soil for new life to begin
In spring for flowers to set in
Daffodil, crocuses and blossom new

After autumn comes winter
White, crunchy snow glistening in the sun
Children sliding, gliding, slipping all around
Laughing, singing, enjoying the seasons on the ground.

By Gurmeet Dhanjal

10
Windy Days

Windy days that nobody wants
Entertaining the people on this earth
Leaves on the trees
Dancing, swaying, waving
To loved ones peeking through their windows
Too scared to venture out
Fluttering, chattering, singing their songs
To the brave few out on their walks
With umbrellas dragging them
This way and that

Windy days that nobody wants
Blowing the old leaves
That have gone from
Green, Red, Orange, Yellow, and then Brown
Reaching the ends of their lives
Falling on earth to decompose and decay
Nourishing the soil
For another day yet to come
Feeding the new life
Yet unseen

Windy days that nobody wants
Gently huffing and puffing
To blow the seeds away
Scattering the dandelions first
Then the sycamore seeds
Propelling like a helicopter
Making a smooth landing far away
Germinating and taking birth again one day

Windy days that nobody wants
Inviting the young and old
With their kites
All different shapes and sizes
All competing with their magnificent designs
Causing a traffic jam in the airways above
Kids cheering and laughing
As their kites soar high in the sky
Taking a sigh of disappointment when they take a dip
And plunge to the ground and ask why

By Gurmeet Dhanjal

11
Early Morning Walk

Early morning walk I took today
To my surprise and delight
My senses were awakened
By the beautiful sounds
Of the chirping birds
Planning their day
In discussion with each other
Of what food to have
And games to play

Early morning walk I took today
I saw two strangers
One with a heavy rucksack
The other looking mysterious
With a Mac and a hat
I wondered where they were going
What they were doing
At the dawn of morning

Early morning walk I took today
I saw a few foxes
Sneaking between the cars

Rummaging through the bins
To satisfy the hunger
Of a new day
With a blink of an eye
They had gone away

Early morning walk I took today
Looking around
I saw the porch lights on
In every house
But not a soul was stirring inside
Cars parked neatly in the drives
I sat down for a few minutes
To take it all in and put everything aside

Early morning walk I took today
I saw the tall trees
With the new buds
Beginning to peek out their sweet heads
Exposing the beautiful colours
Of spring blossoms
And the shadows
Falling on the buildings all around
Of the thin branches
Waiting to be filled with the green of leaves

Early morning walk I took today
I looked up
And saw the beautiful blue sky
With shades of yellow,
Pink, orange, and red
The sun still teasing
And waiting on the horizon
To come out and shine its light
Warmth and feed the plants on the ground

Early morning walk I took today
Time to think of my own breakfast
Toast with butter and jam
Or cereal with milk and a drizzle of honey
Greek yoghurt that is runny
Choice, choices, choices
Just a cup of tea
A smile on my face will suffice today
Until tomorrow I bid you goodbye and ta-ta
For this was the early morning walk I took today!

By Gurmeet Dhanjal

12

Feeling the Loss

Today I lost my cat I swear
Nobody knows where
How and when it happened
Nobody knows
The day was Sunday
The routine was the same
I watered the plants
She played outside
Only difference was
She didn't show up at the door
Regardless of my roar
No scratching on the floor
Like before
To our calls she did not answer
Days went by
Looking, searching
Nowhere to be found
Oh, Cleo
You disappeared
Without making a sound
Left behind a path
Full of pain and sorrow

The neighbours offered their cats to borrow
With reassurance 'She will be back tomorrow'
False alarms we had many
Your match there wasn't any
Oh, Cleo
Where did you go?
Why did you go?
We will never know
It was your time
To leave us we know
You missed us too
You came back to show
Weak and frail
You went off the rail
Looking and searching
For a way back home
Without food and water, you did survive
We were lucky to find you alive
We did our best to revive
The life you still had
In your frail, weak body we did find
But it wasn't meant to be
You came to say goodbye
Now I can see
You had so much love to give
The house is empty
No scratching on the door

The food bowl empty
Litter tray gone
Your bed a reminder
That you did once call this home
For many years
We had so much fun
From climbing the trees
On seeing a mouse, you did run
A bird or two
You killed without a gun
Your present to me
How clever you were
You wanted me to see
A big hole in our heart
You did leave
Now only pictures are proof
Of your existence
In this family
You are missed each day
You were friend and companion
Of the best kind in a way
Goodbye, Cleo!

By Gurmeet Dhanjal

13
How to Keep your Husband/Wife

When I got married
Life did not start
Until one acquired husband or wife
Be he/she of your choice
Or that of your family
One took a leap of faith
Into the unknown
A few boxes did get ticked
He/she will do
Is he/she good looking?
Does he/she have a good job?
Does he/she come from a good family?
Is he/she from the same religion?
Is his/her family from the same village?
Do the surnames match?
What education does he/she have?
These were the questions
matchmakers asked
If the answer was 'Yes'
The deal was done
All it took was £5
To be betrothed

Next the engagement
Wedding date set
Venues agreed
Guest lists exchanged
Gift list made
Photographer booked
Food tasting arranged
Cake selected
Wedding outfits bought
The limousine hired
Best man elected
Jewellery purchased
Makeup artist, marquee reserved
Honeymoon discussed
Loans arranged
Deposits put down
This is what it took to get a husband/wife
I damn well will make sure I keep him/her forever
First love and trust him/her I must
Get acquainted with his/her likes and dislikes
I learn to become the person he/she respects
While standing my ground
We have a plan to keep us together
A couple of children would take us further
Holidays, birthdays, and special events
Choosing schools, attending open evenings
Celebrate festivals

Keeps us going
We learn to support each other
When things get tough
With gentleness and love
We forge our way through the darkness
Of loss, destitution, and legal battles
But one thing that never crosses our minds
Is to leave each other
For life happens
Deal with it you must
What is life without a little action?
We praise each other over little things
The way I look
Or something that I cook
'How did you know that's my favourite thing?'
'Because I know you, darling'
We ignore the things that aren't important
Gives us our uniqueness
Turn a blind eye to what goes wrong
Is the way to keep a husband/wife
It's not easy but we have to be strong
Best things are worth the fight
Each and every day
For the love we feel in return
Keeps us united
Marriage entwining two souls
Travelling the earth together

Departure inevitable one day
But until that day
Love each other we must
Savour the taste of life we have
Count our blessings
To be together
As husband and wife

By Gurmeet Dhanjal

14
Lockdown, Lockdown

Lockdown, Lockdown is all that we hear
Here, there, everywhere,
On the news, in the papers
The conversations we have
Cannot ignore the dreaded word

Mental health and furloughed
The new word's on people's mind
How is your mental state?
Are you furloughed?
Questions that you find

Duties above and beyond
By the NHS staff
Earned them a weekly clap
Free meals and priority passes everywhere
Have now become a trap

People in their homes
Getting creative with cooking dishes
For the hungry and the vulnerable
Kindness is now fulfilling their wishes
GOD must have a bigger plan that we cannot yet see

Giving people time to slow down
Count our blessings and be free
From the everyday hustle and bustle of society
I learn to fall in love with and respect the real me
You can do the same
By shedding the labels stuck on thee

Long walks in the park and a morning jog
Getting inspired by Skipping Singh
A daily workout with Joe is a win
Cosmic Kids yoga
In our living room studio

Taking on new projects never done before
Taught us how versatile we can be
Seeking pleasure from gardening
Enjoying homegrown food
That tastes so sweet

Questions that we ask:
When will things go back to normal?
When will I be able to see my family?
Will I still have a job after COVID?
Is it worth making plans for the future?

GOD's answer I hear:
Create your new normal based on your needs
FaceTime, Skype, and Zoom
Will keep you close to your family
Visualise things you want to appear
Live each day as it's your last
Plan your life without fear

The world as we know it
Has evolved many times over
Why should it not change now?
With new changes come new experiences
That help us grow
Stronger, wiser, resilient, and versatile

So, I say to you, my friends
Do not despair
Live in hope and have faith
For this is the new beginning
Here to stay
Bringing us closer together
Each day

By Gurmeet Dhanjal

15
School Days

Those were the days, my friend
When the world was waiting for us
Playful days and carefree nights
Cramped with reading and homework
To be handed in the next day
When the teachers expected respect
The children had no rights
Except to listen to the teacher
And do as they were told

Filled with fear of parents being told
Of the little things that went wrong
Aiming for the best
And having no rest
While helping Mum with the cooking
Shopping and the rest
Babysitting was a chore without pay
Playing games in the garden
Until the sky went grey

Lunchtime meetings in the park
With the boys for a lark

Flirting, fantasising, teasing
Was a game we played
For the parents never to find out
Forbidden was the teenage love
We did crave
Holding hands, stealing a kiss
Company of friends we did miss

Then the day came for the exams to take
Careers to think about
And a future to plan
With an income to pay the mortgage
And family to support
While our parents looked from afar
With eyes full of pride
'They did well'
For the kids were now settled
With a family of four
Daily duties no longer a chore!

By Gurmeet Dhanjal

16
To My Papa

To my papa, I want to say
A few words I forgot yesterday
Because of you, I learnt to pray
For the things that go astray
I remember your wise words today
As I am faced with dilemmas
Of my children in a way

When you said
'Girls don't do that'
I stood up tall and answered back
'Why not?'
You looked at my determination
And gave in
With a smile
You knew things I didn't know!

Today, as a mother of three
Papa, I can see you smiling down at me
As I go through the
Strong will displayed in front of me
By not one but three

Oh, how I wish you were here
To give me the chance to say
How sorry I am
For the things I put you through

I think you would be proud to see
The daughter you raised in me
The mother I have become
The wife I have learnt to be
Most of all
The things I have achieved
For me
I have finally learnt
To love myself unconditionally!

To my papa, I want to say
A few words I forgot yesterday
Because of you, I learnt to pray
For the things that go astray
I remember your wise words today
As I am faced with dilemmas
Of my children, in a way!

By Gurmeet Dhanjal

17
Reaching for the Stars

The day I was born
I could hear people say
Reach the stars, she will one day
The winning smile
Will melt people's hearts
Can you see the kick she just gave?
That is true strength
My daughter will be a footballer one day
Then again, she has the gift of words
She could be a solicitor
An accountant
A teacher
Or an engineer
But most of all
I want her to be happy
With a husband and a family
Respecting and being respected
Daughter, sister, wife
Mother, a friend of the best kind!
My daughter is born to reach the stars

'Hold on, hold on,' I say

Did anybody ask me or let me have my say?
Yes, I will reach for the stars
But first, I need your LOVE
Support and guidance, if you may
To meet your requirements
But then I have my own plan
To help me on my way
I have come on this earth
With a mission to fulfil
Experiences to have
Please allow me the time and space
To think some more
Make a plan
And work abroad
To find answers by the mistakes I make
Strengthen my character
Stand up straight
Then I will reach the stars one day
Make you proud and go my way!

By Gurmeet Dhanjal

18

My Perfect Valentine

Voluptuous, radiant, red lips
Arrows piercing through the heart
Longing, loving, lustful, love
Eternal, enigmatic, enjoyable, eventful, everlasting bond
Natural, nifty, nourishing, nymphomaniacal connection
Tender, timeless, trailblazing memories
Intimate, intentional, inviting arms
Natural, naughty, nervous gaze
Emotive, elegant, enlightened soul
Sophisticated, splendid, strong will
Devoted, determined, dainty like a bud
Ageless, agreeable, authentic spouse
Yearning, youthful, yes person

My perfect Valentine

19
Sir Tom

There lived a man called Tom
Who really was so warm
To a hundred he did live
Who had it in his heart to forgive
The world he did inspire
In their hearts he ignited a fire
To do what they could
Raise money for good causes
With his Zima frame he did walk a mile
He greeted passersby with a smile
From simple old Tom
The Queen knighted him to become 'Sir Tom'
For all the good he did in a while
Stimulating a wave of applause
A worldwide star you did become
Two hundred and fifty thousand birthday cards
Displayed on the floor without a crumb
Making turning one hundred
A special event
Writing books, giving interviews
Making special appearances
Not a minute you did waste

Of the life that was still left in you
Inspiring children who'd turned five
With stories of courage and strength
Never to give up the fight
In the end, COVID-19 did make you surrender
Leaving mortals on this earth to wonder
What else you could have achieved
If you had lived a little bit longer
We love and salute you
As you enter your eternal sleep
Your kind words
'Tomorrow will be a better day'
Will be a beacon on those dark days
When people have lost faith
And there is the need for a hero
Like you, Sir Tom
Now immortalised
In a statue tall
For all to see
Sir Tom
For now, we bid you goodbye
Rest in peace

By Gurmeet Dhanjal

20

Evils of this World

Poverty
Ownership
Weak
Empty
Retarded

Gagged
Ruthless
Evil
Eruptive
Damaging

Mean
Opposed
Negative
Explosive
Yell

Disgusting
Ill
Scary
Cringe

Regretful
Illegal
Messy
Ignorant
Notorious
Angry
Terrible
Indomitable
Offensive
Need

By Gurmeet Dhanjal

21

A Modern Family

I was born to a loving couple
Otherwise there would be no me
So I ask a question
Why am I torn between
Parents who
Both want to be set free?
One weekend with Daddy
The other with Mummy
I feel like a football
On a pitch
In between I am tackled
With the two families
Who now don't even speak
What am I to do?
With a good talking to
I become wise
I learn how to play
Everybody's game
I am the smart kid
Who is coping
Learning to survive
In this world so cruel

Where children
Are the bait
To fight over in courts
Being made to choose
Between the people who made me
I see my friend's mum and dad
And wonder why
That can't be me
A seed is all you need
My mum tells me
To make a child
But I tell my mum
It takes a village to raise a child like me
When I grow up
Will I make the same mistakes?
I hope not
As a child of an exceptional family
I know the pains
But I understand
They must have had
Their reasons too
So I would just like to say
Mummy and Daddy
Your love I do feel
In different ways
The struggles you endured to have me
I thank thee each day

And wish you both
All the happiness
Coming your way
Your child!!!

By Gurmeet Dhanjal

22

Exceptional Parenting

I saw my friends laughing
No more washing
And cleaning after the man
Who called himself the father
Instead, I have a visiting rota to plan
His weekends
My weekends
Finding babysitters
For when I want to go out
Single parent
No one told me about the lonely nights
I'd have to suffer
Problems to solve
Help me with the discipline
Getting maintenance money
Is a chore
But without it
How can I make ends meet?
I could do with a hug
And a loving word in my ear
But where to go?
Who to ask?

I look for a substitute in a bar
He's alright for a date
But nowhere near to my mate
Single person now I must be
Until one day
My fortunes do change!

By Gurmeet Dhanjal

23

Going our Separate Ways

We are going our separate ways
Is the word
You hear in passing
But one day
It reared its head
And came my way
Happiness is what
I am looking for
So we are
Going our separate ways
The struggle to get there is hard
Emotions all bubbling
Letters to solicitors
And heavy bills to pay
All relationships
Under review
What can I say?
It's hard seeing them
And then walking away
These are the people
I once loved
And they loved me

What's changed?
Tempers died away
Things I dreaded
Nowhere to be seen
Life is a lull
Now that the storm is gone
New beginnings
Is the question on my mind
Where to start and how?
Let the dust settle
And prepare the ground
For new seeds to sow
Look for the buds
Before the flowers will show
Going our separate ways
A unique journey
You came into my life
To make a new person
Of me
Wise, strong, rooted
For the road ahead
Is littered with gems
That sparkle like snow
Divorce is a new word
I didn't know!

By Gurmeet Dhanjal

24
Happiness is Being Served

Happiness is being served
It's finally here
Years of abuse
Shouting and screams
Why was I abused
Like an animal
In a cage
Is it humane?
I ask
To treat another
In this way?
Abandoned and chucked
Like rubbish one day
Happiness is what I seek
For my soul
To find peace
Return what is mine
For I have no need
For what is yours
Take it and make an exit
Through the double doors
Make amends

For the mistakes
You have made
For happiness is coming my way
Nowhere to hide
You have been exposed
Ah…happiness
You taste so sweet
Now with my head
Held up high
With a smile on my face
I begin to live
My life again
Building bridges
Making dreams come true
With my true love
And a family new
Happiness you taste so sweet
Thank you, Thank you
For finally
Showing me this day
Happiness is being served I say
I see the light
At the end of the tunnel
Shining bright

By Gurmeet Dhanjal

25
Bud

Three letter word
Full of hope
Enveloping new life
Nurturing the flower within
Feeding, caring, loving
Until the season comes
For it to be released
First the shoot
Tender green leaves then follow
Sharing a sneak preview
Of what's to come
Blossom of endless colours
Pink, white, purple, and blue
Each day full of surprise
At first the bud
Then the petals
To the beautiful flowers
Titillating and tantalising
All the senses
From the sweet scent
Of roses to the perfume of lavender
Engulfed in the air

That we breathe
Universe now full of life
From the three-letter word called
BUD

By Gurmeet Dhanjal

26
Night Sky

Illuminating the sky
With colours so bright
Yellow, red, purple, and grey
Behind silhouettes of houses standing tall
Like the blazing sun
Spreading its heat
Over the earth below
Stars all hiding
Moon nowhere to be seen
Letting the night sky
Burn so bright
Taking the stage on this night
For the world to see
The amazing sights
Without any lights
Illuminated sky so bright

By Gurmeet Dhanjal

27
Friends

Friends, sisters and brothers
One never had
Like an umbrella on a rainy day
Shelter from the rain
A parasol on a hot, sunny day
Laughing, joking
And playing away
A snug blanket
Keeping you warm
On a winter blistery, snowy day
A shield of iron
Protecting you from
The hailstones
That life throws your way
A soothing hot, frothy cup of Cocoa
When people you love go away
Friends
Lending an ear
Impartial, non-judgmental
Allowing space for stories
Told a hundred times and more
Friends

Turn your upside-down lips
To a smile every day
Friends, sisters and brothers
One never had
Without them it would be very sad I say!

By Gurmeet Dhanjal

28

Trolling

Trolling, a way of life for some
On the Internet they do come
Day in, day out
Terrorising innocent people
And shouting
These are the bullies
Who are so weak
They don't know how to speak
A kind word or two
Instead, their jealousy
Drives them towards a few
Who have the courage
To do something new
A talent they have nurtured
With a focused mind
Hard work that furthered
Their careers
To earn their daily bread
Now live their lives in dread
For death threats
And abuse that follows their every step
Sleepless nights

No end in sight
From this ordeal
Of social media
We hold so dear
A double-edged sword
It has become
Uniting people
And tearing them apart
By those who have no heart
Pulling apart the fabric of our society
Thread by thread
Fuelling relationships
With anxiety
Trollers, take heed
For all this hatred
There is no need
Find a passion
Follow your heart
Give it some love
Be looked down from above
With eyes of love
Enjoy the sweet nectar
Don't be a defector
From society
Come to your senses with **sobriety**

By Gurmeet Dhanjal

29

Snow

Snow is falling
Snow is falling all around
Like a pure, white carpet
Freshly laid down
An invitation from above
To have fun and enjoy
The day away
sledging down a hill
Or building a snowperson
Children rummaging
Through the house
Searching for that
Perfect carrot for the nose
Buttons for the eyes
Orange peel for the mouth
A snow person wouldn't be complete
Without a scarf
And sticks for the arms
Feet crunching on the freshly laid snow
Footprints of the birds
Looking for that rare worm
Foxes leaving their marks

While rummaging through the bins
Desperate to find some food
Hidden beneath the snow
The empty branches
Of the trees in the park
Hosting the snowflakes
Looking down
At the dancing feet
Tip-toeing carefully
On their daily beats
Desperately trying to keep fit
While dreaming of
Hot cups of tea and toast
That await their return
On this cold, frosty, snowy day
Snow is falling
Snow is falling all around!

By Gurmeet Dhanjal

30

WhatsApp

WhatsApp
Here to stay
No question about that
The ting in the night
Disturbing the sleep
While quietly reading one's book
Or cooking your daily meal
The pull of the TING
Irresistible to ignore
Makes one jump
And run to its call
Check all notifications
Lest it be important
But NO
It's a video shared
A hundred times or more
Of jumping monkeys
To the battering of a person
Glorifying the misdeeds of a few
The occasional joke
A welcome distraction
That makes you laugh

And brightens your day
To beautiful reminders
Of the natural beauty unseen
Thousands of miles away
Are connecting us
People of today
Not a voice to be heard
Or face to be seen
Forgotten is the art of
Writing letters in neat
Postcards of holidays
Can't be beat
Of days gone by
Anticipation and joy of the latest news
From loved ones far away
Brought by the postman
With a knock one day
Are all memories of yesterday
Today the connection is always there
WhatsApp
Here to stay
The TING now a welcome sound
Letting you know of people around
Who care to share
A photo or two
Of the family new
The babies born

Marking each milestone
With a video call
Making sure they're not alone
On this journey of life
Through dark days and light!
Making ordinary people into heroes
While turning heroes into zeroes
WhatsApp
Now here to stay

By Gurmeet Dhanjal

31
Old is Gold

Old is gold they say
I would say it's true in a way
Gold stands the test of time
It took a long time to mine
One had to work hard
To dig so deep
Day and night without any sleep
Sifting it through a sieve
For any mistakes
We learnt to forgive
With a little bit of love and care
We did learn to share
The wisdom we found by chance
For others to learn to dance
Today the symbol of gold
Holds memories of old
That gives comfort
Like old beds triumphant
Knowing the rest it does give
For the soul to live
Without a rest
One is not at their best

Helping to maintain the shine
Without a whine
Old is gold they say
To it I say Hooray

By Gurmeet Dhanjal

32
Life Interrupted

Life interrupted
Time to pause
Time to reflect
Time to heal
Time to energise
Time to reset
Time to set new goals
Time to be thankful
Time to forgive
Time to self-love
Time to appreciate
Time to clean
Time to look forward
Time to cut ties
Time to start something new
Time to reach for the sky
Time to let go of fear
Time to be brave
Time to breathe
Time to take the plunge into the unknown
Time to dig deep
Time to be your best friend

Time to make dreams come true
Flip life's interruption
To
Life's Opportunities
You will soon realise
In life there is only change
Never a mistake
Life Interrupted
Comes with an agenda
To us unknown
Waiting for the right time
For it to be shown

By Gurmeet Dhanjal

33
Washing Up

A privilege for a home
That has water
That runs
A luxury denied to some
Dirty water to drink
Bath, wash, and cook without a sink
Exercise for the hands
While rubbing, scrubbing
And washing the ends
Of a meal
Enjoyed by a family
While some escape
This chore happily
For many
It is their duty
To escape it
You are being snooty
Missing out on all that fun
Of playing with water
And then run
To stack up the dishes
Before you get called a sissy

Time for reflection
Before taking any action
On those millions of things on your mind
Look forward to a sit-down
And leave the day's events behind
Now that the washing is done
A privilege afforded to some
Next time don't be afraid to come
To have some fun!

By Gurmeet Dhanjal

34
The Golden Years

These are our golden years
My dear
Like the pebbles on the beach
We did collide together
My love
Washed, scrubbed, and rubbed together
By the hurling waves
My dear
Then dried and sparkled together
By the shining sun
My love
We played games together
With visitors
My dear
On their yearly trip
To the beach
My love
Thrown into the water
And chased by the dogs
My dear
But somehow
We found a way to stay together

My love
These are our Golden years
My dear
Like seeds blown
By the wind
Into the distance
My love
We landed side by side
We learnt to grow together
My dear
With our branches intertwined
We sheltered and fed the hungry
My love
From a bud, flower, then to fruit
Each year
My dear
We found a way to stay together
My love
These are our golden years
My dear
To go for long walks side by side
Without a word
My love
When the grandchildren come
We can play and send them back
My dear
Without losing our sleep

Over what lunch to pack
My love
We can laugh, hug, and kiss some more
And then say goodbye
My dear
Time for us to have a cuddle
And a smooch
My love
We found a way to stay together
My dear

By Gurmeet Dhanjal

35
My Knitting Needles

My knitting needles
You have been my companion
From the start
At times of stress
You brought me calm
With a jumper or cardigan to knit
When waiting in anticipation
You gave me purpose
With designs of matinees
Booties hat and gloves
When loneliness took hold
You became my companion once more
Urged me to get knitting
A jacket and a scarf that touched the floor

My knitting needles
You bring out the creativity in me
Learning new stitches
Through a language new
You taught me about patience
To try and try again
All the different wools

Eager to be wrapped around you
Thick, thin, Aran, and Acrylic
All waiting
To be turned into
Something
That will wrap around and hug
A beautiful soul who is waiting

My knitting needles
You may be just
Two metal spikes to some
But you are part of me
That helped to shape the person
I have become today
I need you more
Today than I did yesterday
As into retirement
I have come
With plenty of time
On my hands to kill
Inspire me, motivate me
Drive others as you do me

By Gurmeet Dhanjal

36
Paronthas

Little did I know
I would become hooked
On paronthas
Cooked by Mum one day
The taste was so yummy
At the mention of the word
The tongue starts salivating
Waiting for the weekend to arrive
Aloo paronthas with yoghurt
Or Methi ones with butter
Ones stuffed with mooli
Are by far my favourite
With a cup of masala tea
Mum, bring out the Paronthas

When away on holidays
Pasta is so bland
With risotto on the plate
Please I want to leave this land
The alternative is a salad
Or soup with a crusty bun
If you are lucky

There might be a jacket potato
With a filling of cheese and beans
Which makes me want to run
I pick up my phone
And dial my mum's number
Mum we are on our way home
What paronthas have you got?

By Gurmeet Dhanjal

37
Valentine's Day

Valentine's Day they cried
On the radio, TV, and social media
Buy your flowers today
At inflated prices
They advertise in all stores
From Tesco to Asda, Morrison and more
Don't disappoint your loved ones
Meals for two
And all the perfumes too
A single rose
To a dozen or two
Are choices made by a few
On Valentine's Day

It makes me wonder
Will the love you show be different?
If it's shown a day too late
And the prices you pay be halved
Over a simple meal of fish and chips
Wrapped in paper plain
Would your love be less?
If you picked a flower from your garden

Or made it out of paper?
Would it make a difference
If the colour were yellow, pink, or blue?

Oh Valentine's Day
Where did you come from?
Who have you come to fool?
For I want to show my love
Not just on one day
But everyday
Not with flowers
But with my body, mind, and soul
Let the perfume
Be the smell of my body
Let the beauty be in the words
I whisper in your ear
Let the food we eat
Be the happiness we share
Not for one day
But an eternity!
Oh Valentine's Day
Make this your promise to me!

By Gurmeet Dhanjal

38

Oh Christmas Tree

Oh Christmas tree
Oh Christmas tree
So glad you're here for me

For eleven months you left me alone
You disappeared without a word
Where did you go?
Who did you see?
What did you do?
When did you decide to come back to me?

Oh Christmas tree
Oh Christmas tree
So glad you're here for me

All year round
We anxiously await your arrival
To brighten our lives
With baubles, stars, and tinsel
Red, yellow, blue, and green
With presents hidden underneath

Oh Christmas tree
Oh Christmas tree
So glad you're here for me

Children crowding around at night
Waiting for the midnight alarm to ring
In a rush scrambling to find their names
Tearing open the wrapping paper
Peeking through the hole
To see what Father Christmas did bring

Oh Christmas tree
Oh Christmas tree
So glad you're here for me

By Gurmeet Dhanjal

39

The Waiting Game

Waiting for this, waiting for that
Why, why, why
I have things to do
Things to say
Places to be
People to see
Experiences to have
Then why, why, why the wait?

My life is passing by
Each minute, each hour, each day
Is deducted from my life
Wait, wait, wait
Is all I do each day
Wait for him
Wait for her
Wait for them
Wait forever

Then one day I realise
Not all things are in my power
There is a reason for my wait

It's to teach a lesson
In patience
For better things
Yet to come
Incomprehensible
By my simple mind

Wait, wait, wait I must
To see the magic
Of the Divine
Who has a plan
Unknown to me
Open my mind I must
To receive treasures
Of the eternal kind
Wait, wait, wait
I will, in delight!

By Gurmeet Dhanjal

40
NuSound Radio

NuSound Radio you came into my life
Like a swirling wind
Where you came from
How you came is a mystery to unfold

I had a wish to share my story
Then an angel flew in
By the name of Mohni
Our lives did entwine
On one International
Women's Day at nine

My book I did give to her
A lift in the car was all it took
For our sisterly love to hook
In awe of each other's work
We did become

Now sharing the airspace each week
Giving voice to silent words
On each page of my book
Bringing my poetry alive

To the millions listening
To our show

With this little poem
I want to say my thanks
To you Mohni for recognising
The worth of my words
To share far and wide

Now that the seeds are sown
Amar Award is in the air
We can multiply my book
A thousand times for people to share
Their story yet untold
We'll slowly watch unfold!

By Gurmeet Dhanjal

41
Enough

Enough says my heart to my mind
To the horrors of this world
To Trump in America
And Modi in India
To Boris Johnson in the UK
And Putin in Russia

My mind is going numb
It doesn't know what to think or do
Hearing the cries of farmers in India
Who fight for their land
To earn an honest living
Sleeping in the cold
Families left behind

My mind is going numb
Watching the news each day
For updates on rules and restrictions
On how to keep safe
Avoid catching the dreaded COVID-19
Government promises to keep us safe
Whilst the NHS struggles
To stay ahead without any sleep

My mind is going numb
Reading the tweets of a madman
Who calls himself the president
Whilst his subjects
Are dying in their homes
And people he calls patriots
Go on a rampage
In his golden cage

My mind is going numb
As I go through the day
Doing all the things I normally would
Having lost its purpose and why
Pondering about the world I am in
When a little ray of sunshine
Comes blasting in
The giggles of angels sent from above
The grandchildren

My mind is going numb
But my heart is full of hope
Watching the future unfold
New life growing around
Bearing new fruit
Without maggots and germs
The fruit we eat full of sweetness
And delight

By Gurmeet Dhanjal

42

Farmers

Farmers of today we salute you
For the food we enjoy each day
Your work never stops
You work day and night
To sow the seeds
Plough the earth
You must

The balance of the weather is key
The sunshine, rain, and wind
Each doing its job
To the bees, caterpillars, and snails
To pollinate, polish, and keep the leaves clean
Farmers out in all weathers
For the love of their jobs

Farmers of Guru Nanak
Now fighting for their land
To fill the bellies of the hungry
While the men in white suits
Want control
To fill the wallets of the few
Already bursting at the seams

Oh you greedy men
Realise before it is too late
That the riches of this world
You cannot take
To your grave
Empty-handed you came
Empty-handed you will go

While the buzz around you gets louder
The world begins to hear
The cries of the hungry
Your head will hang in shame
Give up now
For the blessings of the few
Who call themselves farmers

What will you say to the Lord Almighty
Of the good you have done on this earth?
Your hands already covered in the blood of many
Who could stand it no more
And took their own lives
Their children left orphans
All hope taken away

Oh the governments of today
Listen to the people
Who had some faith in you

For the betterment of this world
For the children of today
Let go of the ego, the greed of yesterday
Awaken your minds—it's not too late
For compassion, love, and joy
Make this a better world for all!

By Gurmeet Dhanjal

43
Puddles

Puddles, puddles all around
Big ones, small ones,
Square ones, round ones,
Puddles of all shape and sizes to be found
After the rainfall
And thundery showers
On the ground
Children having fun
Splashing, kicking,
And throwing stones
Sending ripples all around
Like a mirror
Reflecting the trees
Birds, dogs, and bees
Muddy puddles,
Clean puddles,
Animals to swim in puddles
Puddles, puddles all around
In the parks and streets
Where everybody meets
When the sun comes out
They are nowhere to be found

Quietly evaporating
Into the air without a sound
No mark of their existence
Ever to have been around
Until another rainy day
To start the cycle again in a way
Puddles, puddles all around!

By Gurmeet Dhanjal

44
Mother Earth

Mother Earth
What have we done to you?
Ripped your belly apart
Without a care
As shown on our tellies
From the seas to the forests
Agriculturists to the florists
Greedy to make a profit
Landfills full of waste for a deposit
Overfishing the seas
Bringing the scientists to their knees
Destroying the forests
For their wood
The animals running a mile if they could
Robbed of their livelihood
Nothing left of their neighbourhood
Species lost forever
Despite the last-minute endeavour
By some
Who believe and are in awe
Of your creation
Mother Earth

You feed, nourish, and clothe us
Let us run and have some fun
Before you open your arms
And let us burn
To ashes and become one
Inside your arms
Wrapped around us
Like a warm blanket
Without a sound
Mother Earth
What have we done to you?
Find it in your heart
To forgive
The pain and the anguish
We caused
As the ignorant, small-minded
Creatures that we are
No thought of tomorrow
While we wallow in our sorrow
As we see the climate change
From extreme heatwaves
To devastating rains
Causing no end of destruction
Stopping society from its function
Dams bursting, ice melting
Changing the face of this earth
Provide us with the will

To preserve and restore
The damage we cause
Devastation is your way
To help us pause
Rethink, respect, and respond
To your calls
Mother Earth we hear you
As we turn things around
For a brighter future
For generations to come

By Gurmeet Dhanjal

45
Hands

Two hands
Together make a team
The five fingers on each hand are a family
One hand on the other
Makes a clap
One hand on a cheek
Makes a slap
A soothing balm
On a sore
Leaves people wanting more
A royal wave
To hitch a ride
Put them behind your back
To hide
Entertain the kids
With songs
About bottles, pigs, and sausages
Hands
Our tools for life
For cooking
For digging
Washing and swishing

Clapping to slapping
Pointing to poking
Riding a bike
Rowing a boat
Patting a dog
To stroking a goat
Two make a pair
To have one wouldn't be fair
Our hands
Give us our life

By Gurmeet Dhanjal

46
Water

The tears in your eyes
When you say your goodbyes

Hot water for the tea
You make for me

Bath full of bubbles
To wash away the troubles

Water in the hose
To feed the special rose

Water in paddling pool
To keep us cool

Water in the pond
For ducks to bond

Muddy water in the swamp
For hippos to go for a romp

Water in our bottles
We find in hotels

Water in the sea
Lets all the fish be free

Water flowing down
From a stream

Pure, colourless, without a taste
Quenches thirst in a haste

Water, source of life
For all creatures without strife

By Gurmeet Dhanjal

47
Rules

Rules; an essential part of life
Without them we wouldn't learn how to survive

Rules at home
Rules at School
Rules at work
Rules for games
It wouldn't be the same!

To live by the rules
Is a game of fools

Without them
I can be free
To explore
What lies beyond
That tree

To break the rules
Is to find new tools

To survive
It is essential
For new discoveries
To lead a life
Free of worry

Rules, Rules, Rules
To obey
Is to play a game of fools

By Gurmeet Dhanjal

48
Found

Once I was lost
Now I have been found
At your feet I am bound
With mine firmly on the ground
As I watch
The moon and the sun go around
The sunshine, you smiling at me
The breeze, like a kiss on my cheek from thee
The rain, the sound of your feet
Running to make me free
The snow, the blanket
You spread on my flaws
Once I was lost
Now I have been found

By Gurmeet Dhanjal

49
The Crow

Caw, caw, caw
Caw, caw, caw goes the crow
Early in the morning
Perching on the rooftops
Then with the blink of an eye
Flying through the air
Far above the clouds
Swooping, diving
Feeling so proud
Sending messages
To the family
That food has been found
Gently gliding back on the ground
With a worm he found
Hanging in his beak
He takes flight
To his nest where he meets
Tiny little mouths
Waiting for their feed
Caw, caw, caw
I hear the sound
Of little babies

Thankful for the meal
Dad has found
Caw, caw, caw
Caw, caw, caw
A beautiful sound
In the morning so loud
As you walk through the park
Or on the open ground
Listen, observe, and see
The wonder of the Universe
Who takes care of them, you, and me

By Gurmeet Dhanjal

50
Pride

Pretentious
Restrictive
Idiotic
Disease
Egotistic

By Gurmeet Dhanjal

51
Forgiveness

Forget that which brings you hurt
Onwards and upwards you must go
Remember that people are humans
Give unconditional love
Ignite the light of compassion in them all
Visit the house of GOD often
Empty garbage from your mind each day
Forgiveness is given in this way

By Gurmeet Dhanjal

52
The Sun

Sun, red, yellow, orange, and blue
Shining down on me and you
Feeding the plants
Warming our bones
Full of nutrition
Helping trees with fruition

Bumblebees busy
Searching for nectar
Flying around the fields
Hectare by hectare
Trees full of green leaves
Providing shade from the heat
Sun, red, yellow, orange, and blue

By Gurmeet Dhanjal

53
Diet

Diet, a way of life
Without it we wouldn't survive
Healthy diet
Fast food diet
Calorie controlled diet
Slimming World Diet
Cambridge Diet
Weight Watchers Diet
5:2 Diet
Jane Plan Diet
Noom Diet
So many different diets
All fighting for my attention
To feed a stomach so small
Mind so confused
So much money to be used
The best diet
Is free
Fruit that grows on a tree
Vegetables pulled fresh from the earth
Water that comes straight from a stream
Freshly baked bread, roti, and naan

With daal, soup, and more
Twice a day
Should suffice
To keep me alive
With daily exercise of
The best kind
Meditation for the mind
Walking the muscles for the body
Paint a big smile
On the soul
The perfect diet
For the mind, body, and soul
Make this your way of life

By Gurmeet Dhanjal

54
Pushing Boundaries

Pushing boundaries
Do so at your own peril
Push the boundaries you must
If you fall
Lean against the wall
Until you muster the courage
With enough leverage
To stand tall
Justify pushing boundaries
To yourself you must
Lessons learnt are key
For your growth
Helping your life go forth
Your mind like an ocean
Not yet explored
Possibilities limitless
Your potential waiting to unfold
Your story is not yet told
Push the boundaries
Without getting discouraged
The rewards so sweet
Being told of in every tweet

Of a hero
Who started at zero
Push the boundary you must
At your own peril

By Gurmeet Dhanjal

55
Reading Club

Reading club
A source of comfort
Discussing books
Of all sorts
Once a week
A date is set
Who will read the most?
All the rules having been met
No skipping pages
Even if it takes ages
Each page has to be read
In the evening before going to bed
Recount each detail
I must not derail
Is what my friends expect
I will abide out of respect
Over a cup of tea
For a minimal fee
Each week
That allows me time to speak
Exchange a joke
Giggle and croak

Is my release
If I am to have any peace
Thank you, my reading club
For lighting the bulb
In my mind
Helping to leave all my worries behind!

By Gurmeet Dhanjal

56
Gardening

Gardening is my world
The rewards are untold
So let me tell you
In the garden what to do
Get your shovel, rake, and hoe
Dig, plant, and sow
Seeds for food
For your tomorrow
That is so good
Water them each day
For a little chat they are so keen
From, chili, spinach, and the odd bean
Waiting your arrival
For their survival
Without you they will shrivel and die
Giving you a reason to come alive
On that hot summer day
Rain providing respite in a way
You sit back and let nature
Give a helping hand
While the seedling
Receives nourishment

From above that lands
Until one day
You see the vegetable
That will soon be on your table
Excitement unbearable
Curry, risotto, or pasta bake
Choices are so many
You cannot choose what to make
Gardening is my world
Rewards have now been told
Get out your gloves
Wellies and get involved
Mother Earth is waiting
Try a new kind of dating
Full of love, and care
To a normal date it won't compare!

By Gurmeet Dhanjal

57

Goodbye, *AuRevoir*, Sat Sri Akal

Goodbye to all that was 2020
Sat Sri Akal to all that is coming
As we say our goodbyes
Let's not forget the whys
Why we are here
Why we do everything we do
Why we meet certain people
Why things happen when they do
Why we need to carry on
Why we need to be strong
Why we need to persevere
Why we need love and compassion
Why we never give up on ourselves
Why, why, why indeed
We have millions of reasons
And mouths to feed
With a little break
We have to dig deep
Come back stronger, wiser, and healthier
For now, it is only aurevoir
And not goodbye
Until we meet again
For that special day we do wait
Through sun, snow, and rain

58
Cleaning

Cleaning, a weekly chore
Pleasure that you yearn for more
Music blaring loudly
Buzzing sound of hoover
Drowning every sound around
Under the sofa, over the chairs
Hoover now dancing everywhere
Upstairs, downstairs
Sucking up all the dirt
Like the mess on a shirt
Leaving the house
Free of dirt and mice
The detergent in the water
Magic mop ready to go
Leaving the sweet scent of
Lavender a long time ago
Swish-swash, swish-swash
It flows
Around the corners
Where nobody goes
Cleaning away the dust
Windows now wide open

To let the fresh air in
Getting rid of stale air
That's been there for a week
Now that the house is clean
Put my feet up
With a cuppa in my hand
A smile of satisfaction
I can rest for another week

By Gurmeet Dhanjal

59
Loneliness

Loneliness, a curse
Slowly falls upon us
One quiet day
Young and old
It's a feeling
Easily shaken off
When you talk
Or simply
Step outside your front door
Interact with neighbours and more
Look and listen for
Walking, talking
Laughing, joking
Now feel connected
You see
You're not so affected
By the notion
Of loneliness and disconnection
In the hood you belong
Sisterhood, brotherhood,
Motherhood, fatherhood
Manhood, womanhood

Find your hood
And never let go
Loneliness,
Curse no more

By Gurmeet Dhanjal

60
Homelessness

Homelessness
Being penniless
Without food or drink
At the mercy of others
To be fed
Day and night
Only a bed
With a cardboard head
Quilt wrapped around
To keep the cold out of bounds
Easy prey
For those adults gone astray
Howling winds at night
Give me a fright
In the darkness
There is nowhere to hide
Once I did have a home
I called mine
Belonging to a family of nine
Where did it all go wrong
As I wonder and keep strong
One stormy night I lost my way

Now I am here to stay
No sign of my family
Only strangers walking by
May sometimes say, 'Hi'
Nobody to talk to
Each day that goes by
Homeless, penniless
Would anyone miss me
If I were to die
I ask myself
Oh, why, why, why

By Gurmeet Dhanjal

61
The Royal Family

The royal family
An institution you cannot beat
The queen, head of commonwealth states
Her duties
She takes seriously
Reading all the letters each day
Welcoming presidents of today
Meticulously dressed
Not a hair out of place
Adorned in her military uniforms
On those formal days
Trooping of the colours
Inspection of the guards
Everybody glued to their chairs
To hear the speech
On Christmas day
Words of encouragement
Of all that's happened and gone away
To welcome the New Year full of hope
Tragedies there have been many
Losing Diana
Break-up of Prince Andrew's marriage
To the new revelations of racism

Insensitivity of new blood that joins the family
To be a royal there is no training
The job is hard
To wear an armour of steel
Is what it takes
To be shaped into a royal
The beatings from the press
Criticisms of what you wear
And how you do your hair
Are things that do not get missed
Every word you utter
Will be tomorrow's news
To be a royal is not easy
It's a job that requires training
Support and encouragement
Spending taxpayers' money
On things like honey
Are considered a waste
What would the world be like
Without the monarchs?
A fixture in the world
For centuries
From Tudors to Elizabethans
From Henry the Eighth and King George the Fifth
Royal family
Is it time for a change?

By Gurmeet Dhanjal

62

Now that you are Gone

Now that you are gone
I wonder what you're doing
Where you might be
Who you might be with
Do you ever think about me?

Now that you are gone
I miss the chats we had
The smell of your body
The twinkle in your eyes
And your quivering lips

Now that you are gone
I wonder what life would have been
With you next to me
Sharing the daily chores
Trips to the theatre and dining out

Now that you are gone
All that is left is a memory
Of what we had
What could have been
And all that was unsaid

63
Now that you are Back

Now that you are back
What do you expect to see?
Years have gone by
I am not the same old me

I am a woman with self-belief
Who is in love with herself
Having shed many layers of skin
Now thinks so deep

Things can never be the same
Even though you call me by my name
I am now playing a different game
Rules have changed but the people are the same

Now that you are back
Buckle up for a ride that is new
Second chances are afforded only to a few
Let's fly away with the new wings that we grew

By Gurmeet Dhanjal

64
The Weather Man

Showers, heavy hailstones, and thunder
Blustery, gale winds blowing over the seas
Blanket of black, stormy clouds
Spreading over those hills
Brace yourselves for a storm

Shut your windows tonight
Hold your umbrellas tight
If you don't want to lose the fight
Against the weather, all right

Sunshine will peek through the clouds
But do not be fooled
As the 50-mile winds
Come gushing from the south
Clear weather is on the horizon

For the silver lining
You have to wait
Pot of gold at the end of the rainbow
Won't be too late

By Gurmeet Dhanjal

65
To Feel Alive

Blessed are those with a body
Without it, you wouldn't be somebody
A spirit in the sky
Asking the question why
When is it my turn?
To earth I must return
To experience the life of a mortal
My body being my hotel
In it, I must reside
During the day I cannot go outside
In my body I feel the sensations
Of rain, wind, and snow
What it means to be alive
Now I know
Relishing the sun
Heat that makes me run
Jump into the pool
That keeps me cool
At night enveloped in the arms of a lover
Under the covers
I feel transported to a land new
Which is visited by only a few

The passion so rare
I feel it without care
With abandonment
I let go of my body
Reunited with spirits once more
I jump back in
Through its open door
Sensations leaving me wanting more
This life I never want to let go
Being alive is to be mortal
With skin, muscle, and bones
Blood that runs through the veins
Passing through the heart that it reigns

By Gurmeet Dhanjal

66
When Two Hearts Meet

When two hearts meet
The heart misses a beat
The eyes begin to greet
The lips start to quiver
The body begins to shiver

When two hearts meet
The night becomes day
The day becomes night
When the other is out of sight
The mind begins to fight

When two hearts meet
A minute becomes an hour
An hour becomes a day
One doesn't know what to say
Or do while the other is away

When two hearts meet
There is colour in the cheeks
The bodies look neat

There is a beat in the feet
Now the day feels like a week

When two hearts meet
Suddenly life has a purpose
With a hustle and bustle like a circus
Tightropes to climb
Children to entertain
With no room left in the brain
When two hearts meet

By Gurmeet Dhanjal

67

You are not Alone

You are not alone
On this journey of life
I am with you every step of the way
Each and every day
To wipe your tears away
Holding your hand tight
I will be the beacon of light
To help you glimpse sight
Of tomorrow
Through rain, sun, and snow
When you fall
I will pick you up
Steering you through
The darkest days of your life
Don't lose faith in me
When you open your eyes
You will see
The path I've carved for thee
Littered with rose petals
Love that your eyes won't believe
You are not alone
On this path of life

By Gurmeet Dhanjal

68
Ghosts of the Past

Ghosts of the past there are a few
In my mind they always live
That's nothing new
Disturbing my peace
I want to be released from this disease
Past, you have served me well
Taking care of me
Dusting cobwebs
Letting fresh air in
Helping me to breathe
Grateful I am immensely
Your contract has been exterminated
New tenants ready and waiting
For a little space in my mind
Bringing a freshness of the times
Full of love, laughter, and more
Lifting the weight off my mind
From the past
No longer prevalent
Ghosts of the past
Now released from their shackles
The past is the place

Where you now belong
The present is now mine
Full of peace and contentment
Haunted by you I am no more
Ghosts of my past
In my mind
You live no more

By Gurmeet Dhanjal

69
Ardaas

A prayer
A request
A conversation
With Omnipresence
Of Graciousness
Of Remembrance
For Fulfillment
For Guidance
For Enlightenment
For Forgiveness
For Immortality
For Everlasting Peace
For Unity
For Mercy
Ardaas
A prayer
A request

By Gurmeet Dhanjal

70
What Mama Never Told Me

When I was young
Mama told me
Girls must learn to cook
Clean the house
Hang all coats on a hook
Knit jumpers and scarfs
Without a book
Cut the grass
Prune the roses
Sweep the floor
Wipe it clean
And how to make
Windows gleam
For visitors
I must always be prepared
With snacks and cakes
No expense spared
Dress to the nines
With a smile painted so fine
With a napkin tucked in
We are ready to dine
What Mama never told me was

How to find my happiness
In the clutter of life
How to breathe
When things got tough
How to step back
And not look so rough
How to love myself
And be loved
In its truest sense
Never to settle for second best
Put everybody through a test
To measure their capability
To deal with life's reality
Mama never told me
I was enough for me!

By Gurmeet Dhanjal

71
I am a Bottle

I am a bottle brand new
Came out of the factory
I am blue
Around the conveyor belt I did go
How many times I don't know
Strengthening, testing, polishing
Until I was ready to be filled
By the label of the company that was billed
First the water, then the flavour
Then the fizz for everybody to savour
The lid screwed on tight
Until it's ready to be drunk one night
Slowly the fizz is released
The drinker is now very pleased
With the drink inside
That no longer needs to hide
Slowly sipping away
Until I am empty again
Tossed in the recycling bin
Melted and reshaped
Until I am very thin
I am a bottle empty 'Oh, man'
Ready to go through the cycle again

By Gurmeet Dhanjal

72
Ageing

A process
You can't deny
Like a hill
You start the climb
Reaching the top
Is hard
To get there
You must survive
The pain and hardship
With milestones
You mark along the way
Reaching the top
Feels fantastic
Scars visible from afar
Climb down is now hasty
Slippery, bumpy, and sloppy
Wrinkling skin beginning to show
Of a life weathered
In the sun, rain, and snow
Every step now carefully taken
Destiny now unshaken
Senses that need to be awakened

Each wrinkle and scar
Telling a story
So far
Acceptance
Of the end
Undeniably spoken
Ageing
A process
The beginning of an end

By Gurmeet Dhanjal

73
5 K's of Sikhism

A Sikh—student of self-discovery
Seeker of Enlightenment
Traveller on this earth
With a guidebook in hand
Often getting distracted
By the evils of this world
The 5 vices
Pride, greed, lust,
Anger, and attachment
Each leading to self-absorption
Destruction and weakness
The 5 K's a gift to us all
Granted one day
In 1699
By the 10th Guru of Sikhs
Guru Gobind Rai
Tested the might of his followers
Sacrifice of their head he did ask
His sanity many did question
Which led them to run away
5 strong warriors stood up for the challenge
And said 'For you, Guru Gobind Rai

We are willing to give our best'
On passing their test
Bhai Daya Ram became Bhai Daya Singh
Bhai Dharam Ram became Bhai Dharam Singh,
Bhai Himmat Rai became Bhai Himmat Singh
Bhai Mohkam Chand became Bhai Mohkam Singh
Bhai Sahib Chand became Bhai Sahib Singh
Now stood in front of the congregation
Adorned with a uniform
Of orange and blue
Warrior saint, soldiers
Defenders of honour
With the heart of a lion
Ready to serve
Made to stand out in a crowd
Of a thousand people and more
Empowered by the symbols
Of the 5 K's
Kesh—uncut hair
Kanga—a small comb
Kara—stainless steel bracelet
Keshaira—tie-able undergarment
Kirpan—a sword
Worn by Sikhs all over the world
Through a ceremony of initiation
To wear it
You have the protection

Of the Saint Soldier
Who himself was initiated
And became
Guru Gobind Singh
From Guru Gobind Rai
For ever-present
In everything you do
The 5 K's are a path
To wipe out the five vices
And be reunited
With God Almighty one day
The women being given equal rights
In every way
The freedom of mind
To work, play, and pray
'Kaur' and Singh
Now the new identity
In every Sikh name
For the empowerment of the soul
Belonging to the family
You never feel alone
The Gurdwara, a welcoming place
Smiling faces greet you each day
'Free langar is being served,
Please come this way'
To show our equality
We sit on the floor

We are one human race
Your colour, creed, or religion matters not
As you enter the door
To be in this hood
You are doing pretty good
The five K's
I will honour
Until I am a goner

By Gurmeet Dhanjal

74

I am a Tree

I am a tree that grew so tall
I lived a thousand years
But never grew old
I weather all that comes to me
But don't tell a soul
I like a hug
And stories to be told
I listen very carefully
To your tales of woe
Signs of stress I won't show
Instead I keep on growing more
Spreading my branches far and wide
Providing a place for you to hide
When you feel there is nobody on your side
From a gentle breeze
To shade from the sun I do provide
My roots so deep
I never fall into a heap
I gently watch the world go by
And all the birds flying so high
To make their nest in me
Hidden away in the sky

From the prey
Who try and try
But you are safe with me
I am a tree that grew so tall
Standing still never to fall
Shedding old skin
That people put in the bin
Is a sign of me being free
From the damage I bore
That can't hurt me like before
I am a tree that will live forevermore
Growing in strength
Height and breadth
I am a tree that keeps on giving and growing

By Gurmeet Dhanjal

75
Silence

Silence
A word
An action
Underestimated by many
The power it holds
Hiding a multitude of sins
Or simply holding everything in
Until the time is right to speak
Weakness it is not

Silence
The peace giver
Source of all answers
Hidden beneath
The superficial world
We call earth
Opinions of many
Polluting the mind

Silence
A treasure chest
Waiting to be opened

For creativity of a kind
That very few can find
Full of wisdom
Providing answers
To rule my kingdom

Silence
A weakness it is not
It is a strength
few will possess
With oversized egos
It will not survive
Contentment, self-assurance
Will be your drive
Seek silence
For you to thrive

By Gurmeet Dhanjal

76
My Silence

My silence means
I am tired of fighting
Now there is nothing left for which to fight

My silence means
I am tired of explaining
My feelings to you

My silence means
I don't have the energy
To explain them anymore

My silence means
I have adapted to the changes in my life
I don't want to complain anymore

My silence means
I am on a self-healing process
I am trying to forget everything I ever wanted from you

My silence means
I am trying to move on gracefully
With all my dignity intact

My silence means
I am tired of fighting
Now there is nothing left to fight for

By Gurmeet Dhanjal

CHAPTER 2

NuSound Radio Listeners

Power Of Media
Empowering The Listeners

Poetry is the voice of the heart and soul. One has to experience, see, feel, and hear things to get inspired. The harder the life lessons, the more powerful the poetry. It is also a way of acknowledging reality within yourself, the outside world, and the powers beyond our comprehension in our daily lives on this earth.

It was my privilege and pleasure to share my poems inspired by my life experiences to get others inspired by theirs. The results are astounding. Each poem is written by an individual to reflect deep emotions that are connected with life today, the past, and tomorrow. They are raw and very real, and they come from the heart.

All of the poems in this chapter are contributions made by NuSound Radio listeners worldwide, family, and friends, and they are based on the lockdown, memories of the past, hope for the future, and simple observations of things around them.

It takes a lot of courage and hard work to write anything, and it is even harder to let it loose to be printed in a book, so my humble thanks to all the poets for their contributions.

Seeing the poems in print makes me feel like we have accomplished what we set out to do, which was to bring out the writer in each other and realise our collective potential to keep our spirits high and get us through the darker days and nights of the second lockdown.

Some Comments

(To encourage and inspire the listeners to write, they each received a free copy of my first book, *Our Dance Through Life*. Below are some comments from listeners who received the book and what they thought of the poetry I shared on air.)

'Morning. Loving the show. Lovely poetry. So touching and just simple. So easy to relate to and actually visualise. You can actually turn it into an image. Pass on my regards to my namesake.'

'Good to keep the brain refreshed and express your inner feelings. I will try to keep the poems balanced and not tragic. Actually picked up on a few things with your conversation with Gurmeet. It is how you can turn a negative to a positive experience. Fascinating different perspectives.'

'Good morning, darling. The poems are very refreshing. Gurmeet Ji is an inspiration.'

'Terrific Tuesday presentation by Mohni, specially the interview with one of the great poetess, Gurmeet! Very inspirational poetry by Gurmeet!'

'Awesomely beautiful poetry about Mother.'

'Enjoyed the "Angel" poem. It was really good.'

'The "Lockdown" poem was equally as good, but the "Angel" one was deep and touching.'

'She seems to have gone through a lot in her life, hence writes beautiful poetry conveying her feelings. And her daughter is following in her footsteps.'

'Good morning, Mohni Ji and Gurmeet Ji. I love the show, and poetry is a way of life for lots of people nowadays in this world... all I would like to say is keep up the great work and keep inspiring everyone. Look as far as you can see but seeing beyond your vision is your secret of success.'

'I got goosebumps on listening to this poem.'

'Thank you so much. Love your strength so much. You have done wonders and given so much to the listeners as a precious memory.'

'My heartfelt thanks to Gurmeet Ji as I received her signed book today. I cried just at the acknowledgements. Thank you for the beautiful words of encouragement, too. I wrote a new poem today. Stay blessed. I am so grateful for both of you.'

77
Traveller By Night

Don't be tired, O traveller by night!
Attempt to reach the dawn, not out of sight,
Let your roads be as rough as a screw,
You march on and you will be through.
Your roads may be the darkest in the world,
Do not lose hope but try to be bold.
Your feet, due to the thorns, may perhaps bleed,
Do not stop but increase your speed.
A day shall come; you shall see the light,
The light of knowledge—Omniscience
And Moksha will be in sight.

By Dinesh

78
Balance

We were born walking a tightrope most others
would never know
Carefully balancing sanity between history and home
Dismantled throne, stolen stones, and corner shop jokes
Forgotten science, literature, politics, and poems
Battled identities getting the best of me
Hearing a narrative juxtaposed to my beliefs
How can they rest in peace if the story was never told
If a tree falls in the forest bribe the witnesses with stolen gold
Rock and roll, Coca-Cola and cocodamol
Coast to coast we're rocking false hope and a foreign soul
The story's old with words encrypted and pages are missing
Retold and translated to stop natives listening
It's primitive until we ride the waves of fashion trends
Ignoring past discretions like we're looking through a
one-way lens
Just a sec, where do I belong in this mess?
Exalted Warrior balancing heart and head!

By Shaanvir

79
COVID-19

Oh, hello, COVID-19, you finally came
To penetrate my mind, body, and soul.
Like an unwanted lover to lay with me
In a manner so foul.
Setting my body temperature to a fever so high
Making me delusional and thinking: am I going to die?
Like so many around the world,
I know I am one of the lucky ones,
It's not for me to reason why.
What else is there you can possibly take from me?
My job, my house, my sanity you have snatched from me.
Yet here I am to tell the tale, feeling weary and weak,
With aching limbs and fuzzy head,
Feeling so poorly and meek.
You have ravaged the world and landed at my doorstep too
For almost a year you have held the world in this
awful place of fear,
Each one of us dreading,
Fearing for our lives and that of those we hold dear.
You have taken our loved ones and now you are sitting with me,

To deal with you in my own way,
My body, heavy with fever and unable to fend for myself.
The disease itself,
I can do nothing about as I am compelled to self-isolate,
Making me feel like a leper in this world,
But I know that I am not alone,
At any rate stay in my home or get arrested,
As I will be breaking the law.
Never in my dreams did I ever imagine this new era of a dawn
Whereby an unseen disease,
Manmade or otherwise,
Would rule our lives in this way,
Giving us all time to think and be grateful for another day.
COVID, you need to leave me now,
For the misery you have bestowed,
Like the broken promises made by the one.
That claimed to love me so,
From that I could walk away,
But not before the damage was done.
But COVID, you need to leave me please, enough is enough.
I really don't know how much more I can take,
I know that I am not the only one,
All I can do is pray.
Lockdown—a word I had never heard before,

Now on everyone's lips,
Deep-seated in our core.
COVID, please set me and the world free.

By Parminder

80
Leading Up to Mother's Day

I told my daughter yesterday
I don't want presents for Mother's Day
Why? She asked me taken aback
Let me tell you, do not give me flack!

Things do not mean much anymore to me
Please don't waste your hard-earned money
All I really need to do is to hold you close
I mean it truly, I do, honey

To hug my beautiful grandchildren
Will be my greatest gift of all
It has been so many months now
Then my heart, it will be full

It's just another day of the year
Significant to showing love
To our Mothers dear
The one that we chose when we were above

Patiently waiting in line for our turn
Waiting patiently to be born

Ready to come into the world
To be held and to be yearned

Blessed are those that receive a Mother's love
And Father's love, of course, too
No one knows what tomorrow will bring
You know what you must do

Do not waste another day or year
Let go of the past and move past the tears
Tell your mother what she means to you
Not once a year but the whole year through

By Parminder

81
Fragrance of Spring

In Japan
Strong winds blow
Year's first winds show
Signalling the arrival of spring
Businesses setting up new ledgers
Wiping the slate clean
Of the year gone by
Letting prosperity of the New Year begin

In Japan
The cherry blossom
The queen of all flowers
The yellow of canola
The blue of nemophila
The multitude of colours of tulips
The scent of them all
Carried on the air by the wind of spring

In Japan
April signalling new beginnings
First-term of school
Entrance ceremonies

New teacher
New friends
Mixed feelings
Excitement and nervousness
Hope and anxiety

In Japan
Season of spring full of hope
Time to try new things
Having new encounters
With nature
Old and new
The pink colour of cherry blossoms
Warming our hearts
Watching and supporting challenges
Of the New Year

By Ayaka

82
LOOK

Look as far as you can
Love as much as you desire
Never leave your side
You will be happy to see
That you are never alone
As you are not one
Form but of many
Just look

By Jasvir

83
Note to My Younger Self

If I had worried less about things
And enjoyed the journey more

If I had listened intently to all
And yet still followed my heart

If I had prepared myself for life's troubles
And still enjoyed each bump

If I hadn't had these experiences
I now realise I wouldn't be me at all

By Ritu

84
The Queue

I queued
Summer heat
Or windy gales
I waited
For the food bag

I queued
Patient and waiting
Some looked on to see
My bag empty
My heart hopeful

I queued
My child hungry
My normality changed
My world now different
Nothing moves me now

I queued
Don't judge me
Hunger is real
Nobody gets it
Until you are in it

I queued
They think they know why
Do I really need it?
Now it's a test
Am I in this now for real?

I queued
For respect for eyes to open wide
See me
I am not invisible
A man, a woman, a child

By Ritu

85
I am a Woman

Forget I'm a woman
I'm much more than that
Weaker?
No just another type of strength
Believe in me
Educate me like a son
I will shine like a star
You will be proud
Not of my accomplishments
But of those that will follow in my footsteps…

By Ritu

86
Somewhere

Somewhere she remains
A fragment of my heart
Taken and stored
Hidden away
For when we meet again

The seasons remain unchanged
Without your gentle smile
The flowers grow
But fail to brighten the day

The pain eases with time
It's definitely true
But somewhere
A fragment of my heart
Taken and stored
Hidden away
For when we meet again

By Ritu

87
Happy International Women's Day

Be the strength of a tree
Grow your branches 1…2…3…
Grow so tall that you cannot see
From where you stand beneath
Each branch will bear the leaves
So full lush and evergreen
Link your roots with other trees for
Together you will not rock in the breeze
Cherish the views that you can see
And don't forget to change your leaves
Bear new ones every year
For they will bring new fortunes, hope, and cheers!

By Selina

88

Love not Hate

Don't hate anyone
Say no to hate

Some say:
It's a bio-war orchestrated
Believing this
Humans all over are frustrated

Some say
It's a Third World War fabrication
Experiencing this
All economies are nearing dissolution
And amalgamation

Some say
It's nature's call qualified
Experiencing this
Humans into graves have
Way beyond quantified

Media in 'Sansanaati Khez'
(sizzling press in Hindi)
Reports which country has most cases
As if we are in a 'race'

By Tanvi

89
Fighting the Coronavirus

Coronavirus
For each heart fighting it
With each passing day
Twilight of dusk
Was not expectedly luminous
Aura around us
Soon became pestiferous
Ocean of sorrow
Became strongly obnoxious
Pandemic is a contagious plight
Of humans worldwide
Is atrocious
Children all over are furious

As well are curious
Promising hope to be back
In joy is obvious
Scariest nights
With worst of fright
Now has to bid goodbye
Pressure is tremendously high
To perform our duties

Is everyone's best try
Let's not sit with woes and cry
Let life be with us
In our stride
As one day we will be
Back in the fields
At dawn to sow the happiest seeds
Remember it's darkest before dawn
Just to experience
Future happier lawns

By Tanvi

90
Happy Days will Bloom and Blossom

With each passing day
Twilight of dusk was not luminous overnights
Enveloped earth with dark plight
Fighting thunderous sword fight
Down-pouring arrowed water
Obnoxiously pestiferous
With new dawn cascading
Days of dilemma would be gone

Nectarous downpours on earth will shine
Birds would chirp on parapet,
Inviting new days' butterflies
Honeybees will strike fields to make hay
Lights would smile on darkness in every way.
Branches of trees
Would wear bracelets of flowers
Pleasant season would cast its shower

The same scenery on earth
Will be empowered
Across seven continents
Enveloped by seven coloured rainbows

Streets will smile in a flow
Every courtyard, adorning
The joy of luminous glow
Flowers will bloom and blossom again
With each passing day

By Tanvi

91
Courage

I was in the dark, hidden in a hard core
Knew not what my future stored

My journey started with the seed
Soil and water was the only feed

Stones and rocks won't let me sprout
I made courageous efforts to come out

I faced challenges to see the light of day
And put aside all the hurdles,

I expressed my tiny self to see towards the light
Stood alone between the rocks as majestic sight

Began my journey not knowing where and why
Had to face difficulties but I tried

Don't be surprised to read my story
Just my effort made it history

This courageous seed blossomed as a flower
Thousands of people stop to view me every hour

By Renu

92
Mum's Cooking

When I think of Mum's cooking
And her sumptuous food
I recall the taste even today
Her cooking was the best not just good

I cherish the memories
When she taught me spoon to hold
Feeding me notorious and delicious food
While the stories she told

Gave me all I needed for growth
As well as food for thought
She nurtured me with love, care, and a smile
Promised me rewards if I finished the lot

To go to the heart of someone
Is through the mouth but no other
How should I repay your debts?
I would like to know my mother

The pleasure and satisfaction from her food I get
I am unable to describe
Why my mum's cooking is so good?
The thought of her food makes me cry

By Renu

93
Just Food

When I see the gorgeous food
Streams of water flow
My stomach starts churning
My eyes play to gobble all

Whether be it one meal course
Or be it five
We eat to live or live to eat
In this world just to survive

The whole world economy
Revolves around the food we eat
Thank you God for this bounty
All the vegetation is his treat

Thank Nature's sun and rain
Soil and seeds, fruit on trees
Day and night, we work so hard
Although everything is free

Be it food comfort
Fast food, wrong or right
Whether be it pizza or pasta
Or Indian cuisine delight

Renu

94

The Beauty of Snow

We soon forget the sunny climate
When we behold the snow sublime
All sing a song of beautiful snow
What a magical creation on the earth below
Who laid this white carpet on the ground?
The fall of snowflakes without any sound
Fir tree, bare trees, green and brown
Turning white makes the atmosphere awesomely bright
Watching snowfall gentle and white

This is time for love, peace, and purity
All is calm and everywhere serenity
Making snowman and snowballs we have fun

Soon it will melt with the shining sun
Silent are birds and all creatures worldwide
Waiting for warm weather to come out from hiding
Who is there in the sky that throws the snow?
Who does this variety show, I desire to know
We will soon forget the sunny climate
When we behold the snow so sublime

By Renu

95
Dear COVID

My Mission is not complete on Earth
No one has taught me so much since my birth
You taught me to let go of fear
Shedding light on a new sphere
You made me realise I was often used
And allowed myself to be abused
Your appearance has made me stronger
So I feel a bit bolder
Your presence awakened my Inner Guide
Allowing me to stand tall with pride
It's time for me to plead
Do not let my body bleed
Your fear spiked a steep learning curve
I realise how much I want to serve
Give me time to Heal Mother Earth
In case I don't have another birth

By Renu

96
The Necklace

I cast my eye over
The Mumbai skyline:
'The Necklace' we call it.
Gently resting on
Mother India's neck,
Carrying it so beautifully
She wears it with pride.

By Mira

97
Souvenir

If you told me to bring
You back a souvenir
From my country
What would I bring?

I'd like to bring you some
Of the pink from the
'Pink City', a nice colour to
Paint your walls

Or some of the
Wonder that makes the
'Taj Mahal'
Seventh 'Wonder of the world'

I could bring you back
The tune that keeps the
Country pulsating, dancing
On its toes.

Or a poem that would
Cover every inch

Of a rhythmic country
I call home

How about a piece of land
In which you taste
The intense heat of an
Appetising nation?

By Mira

98
Holi

*(The festival of colours celebrating the arrival of spring.
People play holi by throwing colours on each other)*

A lady stands in the doorway
Watching, scrutinising
Her robes, crisp and white
Like they've just been taken
Off the washing line

She holds bitterness against
The coming of spring
Flowers, warmth, light
Her world colourless
Like her anaemic face

Washed out, colours have faded
Been buried in her world
An amalgamation of
White and black and white
The trees, flowers, grass

Have all been iced over
Why embrace spring
Like she embraced him
He is dead
He took a part of her too.

By Mira

99
Gauri

(Our Calf in India)
When you slice your fangs
Into your beef sandwich
I think of *Gauri*, grazing
In our *kheti, Junagadh*

Not being able to suckle
On *Ma*
Or feel the warmth of her breast
Her heart pulsing against
Miniature me
Gauri became my donor

Her milk flowing
Through my veins
Nourishing my bones
Strengthening my teeth

To see your teeth
Chomping on chunks of beef
Makes my stomach churn
All the while I imagine

You gnawing
On your surrogate mother

By Mira

100
Battle of the Spices

When *Ma* used to cook
The ingredients came alive
Immersed in the fiery *ghee*
Cumin seeds popped, burnt, and jumped
Out of the pan
Onions gave out a cry of pain,
Softening, caramelising
The spices battling, each wanting
To give a fuller flavor
In the end it was the *bhaji* that put
Out the commotion
Ma waits for the elements
To integrate
Come bubbling to the surface
I taste the landscape
The traditions of my motherland
Are still alive in me today!

By Mira

CHAPTER 3

Aria K Dhanjal

As a teacher, I have spent my whole life trying to motivate and inspire pupils to write. Trying to teach them the techniques has often been a stumbling block as they struggled to fit their writing into the model being taught. Poetry is a language of the heart and mind; therefore, there is no structure required to express what we feel, see, experience, hear, and do. This is exactly what I encouraged my seven-year-old granddaughter to do, and the results were amazing as I hope you will agree by reading her poems in this chapter.

Seeing a book with my name on it was an inspiration that began her journey of writing, drawing upon her own life experiences, feelings at being homeschooled and enduring months of lockdown.

Writing poetry provided a medium for her to deal with frustration, loss, and appreciation of what she still had in life.

The lockdown provided adults with an opportunity to reconnect with nature by getting their wellies on and taking their children and grandchildren to the park and forest in all kinds of weather whilst still following government guidelines and keeping safe.

As the months elongated, so did the frustration at being homeschooled, as children began to miss contact with their teachers and peers and that daily routine of playing, working, and saying goodbye at the end of the day. Zoom calls became the norm, now providing the only link between home, school, and friends.

The positive that came out of homeschooling was the strong bond children were able to develop with parents and the extended family, which would otherwise be minimal and only during school holidays.

Aria's poems take us through a journey from a child's perspective of events through the year from spring to Christmas and all that happened in between.

It was my privilege to watch Aria being announced as one of the winners of a competition run by Conscious Dreams Publishing for her poems about spring, at grandmother's house, and a walk through the forest, a real accolade for a seven-year-old child.

Since going back to school, Aria has received more recognition for her poetry from her teachers and Head Teacher for her creativity, vision and passion for self-expression through her poems. I have included a few of them in this book.

101
Spring

Soft petals peeking through the buds
Painting pretty pink blossom
Raining showers dropping gently on the ground
Indoors feeling joyfully sipping a cup of tea
New life is everywhere
Gorgeous plants blooming in all colours
Toes touching the soft wavy grass
Inviting friends to come and have fun
Mother Nature showering love
Everlasting joyful life cycle

By Aria

102

Snow

Stomp, crunch, smash
Walking through the thick heavy snow
Shining, glistening glow
Foot trails of animals
And people
Making pretty patterns
Children laughing and playing in the cold
Building snowmen, sledging down the hill
Red rosy cheeks and noses
Shivering and shaking
After a long day in snow and sleet
It's time to go home
Then come back tomorrow
For fun and more

By Aria

103
Presents

Mothers and fathers
Go zipping past the shops
The presents go stack, stack, stack
The children keep asking
'When is it Christmas Day?'
Santa comes and fills the stockings
And eats mince pies
Drops off the presents and says, 'Goodbye!'
The children come dashing out of bed
At one o'clock in the morning
And ask, 'Is it present time?'

By Aria

Christmas Tree

Popping lights in your face
All the baubles go clink, clink, clink
Children come zipping past
Wanting to open their presents
The twinkling star twinkles in your face
The children say
'When is it Christmas Day?'

By Aria

105

Lockdown

Oh lockdown,
You've put misery and a frown on my face
I feel like I'm in a prison
"What are we to do today"
"The same old thing for a week"
No friends
No teachers to call my name
No more freedom
No playing in the playground
And shouting to my friends
Feeling unloved
Sitting alone at home
Oh lockdown
You've put misery and a frown on my face!

By Aria

106
Walk Through the Forest

Crunch, crumble
The leaves are talking to me
A walk in the forest
Reminds me of a jungle
Smash, 123
A falling tree
A pool of fresh mud
Oh, watch out!
Splash
Foxes running by
Chasing their next meal
I hope it's not me
At the fountain we have come
Oh no
Piranhas
Let's all run
A fun day at the forest
We did have
Splash, splosh, through
Wet, soggy mud
Now I can't wait to fall into bed

By Aria

107
Friendship

Laughing, loving, having fun
That's what friends do
Caring, sharing, full of mischief
Playing Barbies, making dens
Sneaky snacks
In middle of the night
Squealing, chitter-chattering
Making plans
Doing makeovers
Drawing, colouring, making food
Changing clothes, feeding dolls
And having fun all day
In our unique friendship way

By Aria

108
Homeschooling

Tap, beep, blorp
Just tapping away on the computer
"Oh, no, I missed my Zoom call"
"Honey, are you done yet?"
Mummy calls out
"No, 3 more lessons"
Type, beep, blorp
Just the most boring day ever
Bad for my mental health
I heard them say on TV
No friends to have fun
Or a mile to run for my daily exercise
No Friday STAR assembly
Singing Happy Birthday
To look forward to
Sitting and chatting with friends at lunchtime
Or saying goodbyes at the end of the day
Are now a thing of the past
Can we go back to school soon?
PLEASE!!!!

By Aria

109

Winter

Windy air,
Breezing through the trees
Just let me be

In the house
It's nice and toasty
While outside airy and open

Night is cold
Better get comfy
Let's watch some movies

Tears dropping
From the sad sky
It's all snowy and wet

Even though I shiver from the coldness
My heart keeps me warm
And my love of snow still remains

Really I love the snow
But my question is
'Do you like snow?'

By Aria

110

At Grandmother's House

At Grandmother's house
Everyone rushing around
Doing this and that
While the children
Play with their games
My grandma says
'Let's cook for Mummy and Daddy'
Sizzle, squirm go my eyes
While time on the oven goes
BEEP, BEEP. BEEP!
After a long day at Grandma's
Mummy and Daddy
Come to pick me up
'Time to go home
Say bye-bye to Grandma and Grandpa'
'But I don't want to go home'
I moan
'You will come back soon'
'She has been good as gold'
Chuckles Grandma
'Please bring her back soon'
Shouts Grandpa from afar

Vroom, vroom, off we go
While Grandma and Grandpa
Are waving goodbye
Until out of my sight
What a fun day I had
At Grandma's!

By Aria

111

The Coming of the Iron Man

The iron man stood at the brink of the cliff
Tall as a house, all rigid and stiff

He flashed his great iron eyes
While he thought of eating a few pies
He lifted his huge iron head
Like he was getting out of bed

The sun rose
He could smell something with his nose
Iron man could hear the town
There was a clown

Was it him?
It was Tim
His idea grew
He knew!

He was in a hiding spot
His stomach was in knots
The day flew, flew and flew
He heard a MOO MOO MOO!

He was looking for some metal
All he found was an old kettle
He didn't have lunch
So he munched

He leapt
And so he slept
He was still thinking about pie
While he lay down, feeling sly.

By Aria

112
People Need People

People need people
To be together
No matter the weather
I'm busy
While I'm fizzy
People will always need people
To cry
To rely
To talk to
To walk to
It's useful to have other people around
To be buddies
To study
To play
To lay
People will always need people
To make me happy
Not yappy
Some may have a pony
Then to be lonely
People will always need people

By Aria

This poem was written by Aria during English lesson at school and the inspiration for it were the few lines at the beginning by Benjamin Zephaniah.

Acknowledgements

Thank you to the team at Conscious Dreams Publishing for your commitment and belief in my books. Thank you to Danni Blechner—Book Journey Mentor; Elise Abram—Editor; and Amit Dey—Typesetter, for putting the shine on the final version of this book.

I am grateful for all of my life experiences and to all the people who have come into my life or departed from it. You all gave me material to write about. I am grateful for being the best version of myself and my inner strength that helped me strive under all of the uncontrollable situations with which we are faced each day of our lives.

My heartfelt thanks to Tari Ji and Mohini Ji at NuSound Radio for believing in me and giving me the opportunity to share my poetry on the air. You gave me the opportunity to learn the art of radio presenting, conference calling, sponsorship, and developing confidence in myself to go on air worldwide. My thanks to all the listeners who sent in their messages of appreciation and comments by calling, texting, or emailing from all over the world. My gratitude to those who were inspired and wrote their own poems to take pride of place in this book.

Thank you to all of my family and friends who have embraced me as a poetess and an author above all of our different relationships. Not to forget all of my nearest and dearest friends who actually read my books and took the time to write reviews and scored them out of 5. I am humbled by your kindness. You know who you all are.

Thank you to my daughter, Ravneet, daughter-in-law, Kamaljeet, and son, Harminder, and granddaughters, Aria and Lela, for their everlasting inspiration. Thank you to Dharminder and Nicky for being amazing parents to Aria Dhanjal. Without your love, encouragement and support, her poems would not be possible. Aria through your poetry you have really shown your potential to be an amazing writer of any genre you choose. I cannot wait to see your first solo book being published soon. You make us all so very proud each day. Thank you to my husband for always being there no matter what.

About the Author

Gurmeet Dhanjal is a retired teacher and author. Her passion has always been to help and inspire others. Living in the suburbs of London, she enjoys spending time with nature. In her free time, she enjoys gardening, reading, and cooking.

Aria Dhanjal

Aria is a seven-year-old poet who loves outdoor activities like cycling, going for long walks in the park with her family, and reading. She wrote her first poem when she was only six years old, one rainy day when she was visiting her grandmother. Since then, she has been inspired to write lots more poems. She has enjoyed sharing her poems with her family and friends as well as appearing on NuSound Radio. She has earned many accolades for her poems at such a young age. Her wish is to one day publish a book under her own name. We have no doubt she will do that very soon.

Other Books by Gurmeet Dhanjal

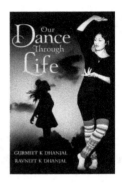

Our Dance Through Life
By Gurmeet K Dhanjal and Ravneet K Dhanjal

In this book, mother and daughter take the reader on a journey of their lives through some beautiful poetry. All heartfelt, some humorous and funny, others exploring deep feelings brought on by events of life about school, loss, love, and the importance of family. This book is truly a conversation from one soul to another written in simple language, helping the reader visualise everything in their minds.

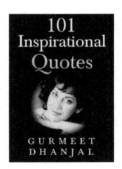

101 Inspirational Quotes
By Gurmeet K Dhanjal

101 Inspirational Quotes is a book full of wisdom and wonderful quotes to evoke change. Everything starts with a thought; if we can change our thoughts we can change our lives forever. Gurmeet Dhanjal believes that we are the creators of our own destiny. The quotes alone cannot do that but they can provide inspiration and act as a catalyst for change. Are you ready for change? If so, this book is for you!

Book Reviews

Our Dance Through Life

"A set of brave and insightful poems capturing some precious moments in life's journey tackled with honesty, emotion, and courage." 5/5

Meena

"I would recommend this book to anyone who loves poetry. Written by some incredible women, I couldn't put it down. A beautiful book." 5/5

Brenda

"An insight into the minds of beautiful souls. Captivating and motivational from the moment you turn the first page. Both books really enlightened my mind frame not only to allowing myself to think more positively but to understand how this was possible too. Happiness and smiles carry you through hard times, spiritually and wholeheartedly. Together and with a smile anything is possible, each day at a time. Thank you for such inspiration."

Carl

"A wonderful snapshot and insight into the authors life through poems and beautiful pictures. A great read!"

"Wonderful reads, highly recommended!" ⚘

Anonymous

101 Inspirational Quotes

"*101 Inspirational Quotes* had all listeners of NuSound radio ready with their pens and papers to write them down as Gurmeet shared them each week. The quotes have been embedded in everyday life experiences, which helps clear misconceptions about life and tweak our thinking to make little changes to live better lives."

Views expressed on air by Nusound Radio listeners.

"This book is full of positive and uplifting quotes; a great way to start the day with a positive attitude. Well written book." 5/5

Brenda

Conscious Dreams
PUBLISHING

Be the author of your own destiny

www.consciousdreamspublishing.com

info@consciousdreamspublishing.com

Let's connect

CPSIA information can be obtained
at www.ICGtesting.com
Printed in the USA
LVHW050046201021
700931LV00010B/503